D0040984

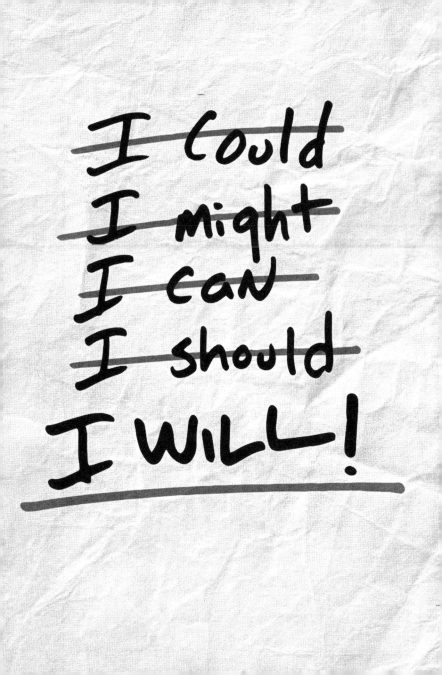

## Other Books by Thom S. Rainer

*Autopsy of a Deceased Church*
*I Am a Church Member*
*The Millennials* (coauthor)
*Transformational Church* (coauthor)
*Simple Life* (coauthor)
*Essential Church* (coauthor)
*Vibrant Church* (coauthor)
*Raising Dad* (coauthor)
*Simple Church* (coauthor)
*The Unexpected Journey*
*The Unchurched Next Door*
*Surprising Insights from the Unchurched*
*Eating the Elephant* (revised edition) (coauthor)
*High Expectations*
*The Every Church Guide to Growth* (coauthor)
*The Bridger Generation*
*Effective Evangelistic Churches*
*The Church Growth Encyclopedia* (coeditor)
*Experiencing Personal Revival* (coauthor)
*Giant Awakenings*
*Biblical Standards for Evangelists* (coauthor)
*Eating the Elephant*
*The Book of Church Growth*
*Evangelism in the Twenty-first Century* (editor)

# I could
# I might
# I can
# I should
# I WILL!

## NINE TRAITS OF THE OUTWARDLY FOCUSED CHRISTIAN

## THOM S. RAINER

**B&H**
PUBLISHING GROUP
NASHVILLE, TENNESSEE

978-1-4336-8729-7


Published by B&H Publishing Group
Nashville, Tennessee


Dewey Decimal Classification: 248.84
Subject Heading: CHRISTIAN LIFE \ HELPING
BEHAVIOR \ INTERPERSONAL RELATIONS

1 2 3 4 5 6 7 8 9 • 21 20 19 18 17 16 15

To
William Thomas Rainer

My Grandson

I can't wait to see you again in heaven.

〜〜〜〜〜〜〜〜〜〜〜〜〜

And always to

Nellie Jo

My Wife

I can't imagine life without you.

# Contents

# Acknowledgments

I love local churches.

I know. There are no perfect local churches, pastors, church staff, or laypersons. But I am so grateful for all those who serve in these congregations. They are the mission points God has given us to share the gospel.

So I write this book with deep gratitude to and acknowledgment of those who are serving on these front lines of ministry. Many people complain about what's wrong with our churches. These men and women labor day by day for the gospel. They are what's right with our churches.

Thank you "Team Rainer" for all you do to make my world of ministry a joy. You three—Amy Jordan, Jonathan Howe, and Amy Thompson—are among the hardest workers I know. You do it with joy and gratitude. My life is richer because of you.

I stand amazed at the B&H Publishing team. B&H has been under the incredible leadership of Selma Wilson and Cossy Pachares for several years. It has been amazing to see God use these leaders to transform an organization. Both have been promoted to other leadership positions at

LifeWay. Their promotions are past due and well deserved. A huge thanks as well to Jennifer Lyell. She is my editor, but she also leads trade books for B&H. I have worked with Jennifer in two organizations. She is one of the most gifted people I know; and I am so grateful she chose to come to LifeWay several years ago.

If you know me in even the most casual way, you likely know how much I love my family. You know how much they are an integral part of everything I do. You know how I depend on them and absolutely adore them. They are a numerically growing bunch, seventeen at present count. There is my wife, Nellie Jo. There are my three sons and their wives: Sam and Erin; Art and Sarah; and Jess and Rachel. And of course, there are my nine grandchildren: Maggie, Bren, Nathaniel, Joshua, Canon, Will, and Harper. If you only counted seven grandchildren, you are correct. Two more are due close to the release date of this book, so I don't know their names as I write these words.

To you the reader, I owe you more gratitude than I can ever express. Some of you have been with me for all twenty-five books. I am ever humbled that any of you readers consider my writings worth reading.

It is my prayer that *I Will* will be an encouragement for you who serve in churches and for you who love the bride of Christ. Though many churches struggle, I remain an obnoxious optimist about their future. I hope you will hear my optimism. And I pray you will have the same hope too.

Thank you for reading this book. And thank you for your willingness to read it with great prayer. It is my prayer that the Holy Spirit will do an amazing work in congregations around the world, and that more and more of us will respond to His call to obedience by saying, "I will."

# Introduction

# A Tale of a Joyous
# Church Member

**H**er name is Heather.
  Heather is a single mom with three kids, two boys and a girl. The ages of the children are five, seven, and ten. Heather is concerned about her children because of the divorce, because they are struggling in school, and because they are failing to obey at home. Yet she has not taken them to church in more than three years.

The divorce was messy. But then again, divorces are not neat and joyous situations. When Dan and Heather split almost four years ago, Heather decided to leave the church. Her ex-husband was staying at the church with his soon-to-be wife. It just would not work for Heather to be around them.

So she left Resurrection Community Church.

And she has not returned to any church for more than four years.

Heather's friends and family sympathized with her regularly. "Poor dear, you lost your husband, many of his

1

friends, and the church you love," some would say. And Heather nodded her head, receiving the condolences with quiet acceptance. It's okay with her if they feel that way.

But Heather has a secret, a secret she has confided to no one. Yes, the divorce was incredibly painful. Yes, so much of the change for her and the kids hurt deeply. Still, she has told no one the full story.

Heather was glad to leave Resurrection Community Church. Indeed, she had become really miserable at the church long before the marital problems began. Leaving the church was one of the blessings of her life changes. It was a big relief.

In order to understand Heather's sentiments, we need to take you back about twelve years ago. That was when Dan and Heather were married. They bought a home where Dan was working. And they both made a commitment to get involved in a church. They mutually decided it would be Resurrection Community Church.

That's where this story begins.

## I Am Not a Happy Church Member

From Heather's perspective, Resurrection Community Church was an easy choice. Dan and his parents had been members there for many years. The church had about 250 in worship attendance. Obviously, Dan knew most of the members. The church members were friendly to Heather as well. They accepted her immediately. After all, she was now part of Dan's family.

Heather really did not have to do much to get involved. Within a few weeks of joining, she was asked to be in a women's

Bible study, to help with the church finances since she was a certified public accountant, and to be a greeter.

When the children came along, it was pretty natural for them to connect in the church as well. Dan and Heather had many good relationships in the congregation. Some of them were young parents with children of similar ages to Dan and Heather's.

So she began church life just fine. Her attitude was great. Her relationships were solid. Her involvement was good.

She has trouble remembering exactly when the change took place. It was more gradual than sudden. Heather, just a few years later, had become an unhappy church member. There was no one negative event. Indeed, she barely noticed the change day by day.

Heather does remember waking up one Sunday morning with a dread about attending church. *When did these feelings develop?* she asked herself. *Why am I no longer a happy church member?*

This story is Heather's story.

But it can be repeated in the lives of church members by the millions.

## The Attitude Shift

Depending on your perspective, you could say that Heather had an advantage. She did not have to wait or seek permission to get involved in the church. Through Dan and his family, she had immediate connections and immediate acceptance. It was as if she had been a member of the church for years.

It was fun for her at first. She loved all the relationships she developed in the church. The members were good people. They took care of one another.

Heather did not attend a church business meeting the first six months after she joined. The church treasurer, though, asked her to attend since she would soon become the assistant treasurer. She needed the background and the experience.

She thought it was strange to have a business meeting every month. But she honored the request. The meeting was nothing like she had expected. The treasurer gave his report, and six or seven church members asked questions about almost every dime of expenditures.

Then the pastor made a presentation to change the worship time from 11:00 a.m. to 10:30 a.m. His logic was sound. The 11:00 time was really late, and it had no obvious benefit. It was just the way the church had always done it.

The opposition was pretty intense. The pastor politely suggested that the change might appeal to younger families who are not members of the church. They often prefer to eat before noon, especially if they have children. Betty, a long-term member, was quick to speak. "I don't know why you're always talking about people who aren't members of this church. This is our church, and our needs come first," she said without hesitation.

The pastor heard the chorus of "amens," and he saw several heads nod affirmatively. He knew the issue was dead. He took the idea off the table.

The pastor would leave the church eight months later. He barely made it to his second anniversary at the church.

In the past twenty years, the church has had eight different pastors. Only one pastor made it to four years of tenure.

Heather would soon fit in with the longer-term members. From them, she learned that church was mostly about getting her needs met. She would often join the chorus of critics when anyone suggested change in the church. Though she would not admit it or articulate it, she really began to view the church as a religious country club that was very careful about letting outsiders in.

You see, Heather joined the church expecting to make a difference. She became a part of the congregation expecting to give and to serve. That is where she found true fulfillment.

Sure, Heather's church experiences were enjoyable initially. She enjoyed at the onset being a part of a club where she was included and others were excluded.

But that self-serving behavior and attitude provided no true fulfillment. When she woke up one Sunday morning with dread and angst, it was the culmination of months of a haughty attitude and selfishness. It was the result of being inwardly focused instead of being outwardly focused. It was analogous to the child who eats too much ice cream and gets sick. It was all about her needs, her desires, and her selfishness.

Heather was spiritually sick and she felt it.

So when the divorce was finalized, leaving the church was the easiest thing to do. She never told anyone how relieved she was to get away from such a self-serving place. And she had no desire to go back to a church. She was done.

## A Time to Return to the Body

Four years passed. Heather was getting restless. The intense pain of the divorce had eased. And she knew something was missing in her life. She realized that as a believer in Christ, she needed to find a church to connect with other believers. For certain, she needed to get her kids back in church.

So the single mom became an unchurched person looking for a church home. Heather began her quest with high hopes, but they were soon dashed.

She told a neighbor "none of the churches have their acts together." There are obvious problems in all of them, she observed.

She reluctantly agreed to a visit from the pastor and his wife from a church she and the kids had visited three times. From her perspective, that church was the best of the bad choices. But Heather would be ready for them. She had the perfect article to show them.

Jordan and Megan, the pastor and his wife from The Church at Fountain Hill, arrived promptly at Heather's home. After exchanging pleasantries, Heather spoke. "Pastor Jordan," she began, "let me get to the bottom line. I have been out of church for four years. I have visited a ton of churches with a good motive to return. Frankly, though, I can't find a decent one to go to. The Church at Fountain Hill is the best of them, but your church has its problems."

Jordan and Megan were patient and kind. You could tell they had heard similar stories. Megan spoke: "Heather, what have been your bad experiences? I think it would help us to know some specifics."

"I thought you might ask," Heather responded. "I saw a blog post this week called 'The Top Nine Ways Churches Drive Away First-time Guests.' I made a copy so you could read it. I have experienced every one of these nine ways at the churches I visited."

Jordan and Megan read the blog post together. The author was brief and to the point:

## Top Nine Ways Churches Drive Away First-time Guests

1. **Unfriendly church members.** This response was anticipated. But the surprise was the number of respondents who included non-genuine friendliness in their answers. In other words, the guests perceived some of the church members were faking it.

2. **Unsafe and unclean children's area.** This response generated the greatest emotional reactions. If your church does not give a high priority to children, don't expect young families to attend.

3. **No place to get information.** If your church does not have a clear and obvious place to get information, you

probably have lowered the chances of a return visit by half. There should also be someone to greet and assist guests at that information center as well.

4. **Bad church website.** Most of the church guests went to the church website before they attended a worship service. Even if they attended the service after visiting a bad website, they attended with a prejudicial perspective. The two indispensable items guests want on a website are address and times of service. It's just that basic.

5. **Poor signage.** If you have been attending a church for a few weeks, you forget all about the signage. You don't need it any more. But guests do. And they are frustrated when it's not there.

6. **Insider church language.** Most of the respondents were not referring to theological language as much as language that only the members know. My favorite example was: "The WMU will meet in the CLC in the room where the GAs usually meet."

7. **Boring or bad service.** My surprise was not the presence of this item. The surprise was that it was not ranked higher.

8. **Members telling guests that they were in their seat or pew.** Yes, this obviously still takes place in some churches.

9. **Dirty facilities**. Some of the comments: "Didn't look like it had been cleaned in a week." "No trash cans anywhere." "Restrooms were worse than a bad truck stop." "Pews had more stains than a Tide commercial."

Jordan had actually read the article earlier in the week. It was written by an obscure blogger who gained a lot of attention with that single post. But Megan spoke first.

"Heather," she began. "That's a good article. We leaders in churches can certainly heed its message. But you could be viewing church the wrong way. Maybe you should not be asking what you can get out of a church, but how God would have you serve through a church. Instead of saying 'I want,' consider saying 'I will.'"

Heather was obviously agitated by Megan's comments. She tried to maintain her composure, but she was clearly bothered by those words. The exit of the couple could not have come sooner.

*Why did those comments bother her so much?* Heather wondered after they left. *Am I really that sensitive?*

## The "I Will" Church Member

Heather slept fitfully that night. She kept hearing Megan's words: "Instead of saying 'I want,' consider saying 'I will.'"

At one point, she opened her Bible. She had just begun reading through the book of Philippians. This time, these words from Philippians 2:3–4 jumped out at her: "Do nothing out of rivalry or conceit, but in humility consider others as more important than yourselves. Everyone should look out not only for his own interests, but also for the interests of others."

"Oh my goodness," she muttered to herself. "That's it! That's why I was so miserable at Resurrection Community Church. I focused on my wants and needs. I did not focus on serving others."

Heather also realized that she had been very critical and picky of churches she had been visiting. She was looking for her wants instead of being willing to say, "I will."

She returned to visit The Church at Fountain Hill. Her perspective was totally different this time. She knew that no churches were perfect. There would always be room for improvement. But now she would, in God's power, serve others first. Her own personal motto became, "Don't say 'I want,' say 'I will.'"

Heather joined the church with her children. She became a joyous church member. Her life became a testimony of "I will." She served with a sacrificial spirit. When other church members frustrated her, she committed to pray for them and forgive them. After all, Christ did that for us at a great cost. It was the least she could do.

Even more, she became an "I will" church member without feeling legalistically obligated or burned out. When she served, she served with joy.

## From Her Story to Your Story

The first few pages of this book were about Heather. The rest of the book is about you, a believer in Christ and a church member. It is about learning how to have complete joy in your service through your church. It is about becoming a fully functioning member of the body.

It is about saying, "I will."

A few years ago, I wrote a book about being a part of the body of Christ, or about being a joyous church member. *I Am a Church Member* became one of the best-selling books in its genre. Its theme was basic: What attitude should I have to be a biblical and joyous church member?

We now move to the next and critical step of being a part of the body of Christ. We move from a right attitude ("I am") to right actions ("I will").

It's really basic. It's a matter of learning what the Bible says about being a part of the body of Christ. It's about hearing His voice through His Word.

And when Christ asks you to serve Him and others in His church, you should have one joyous response. Of course, by now you know the response.

"I will."

## *Points to Ponder*

1. Why do so many church members have a critical and negative view of local churches?

2. How are some local churches acting like a religious country club?

3. Read Philippians 2:1–11. Discuss how that passage relates to being a sacrificial church member.

4. How does the right attitude of church membership naturally lead to the right actions of church membership?

## Chapter 1

# I Will Move from "I Am" to "I Will"

It was one of the best days of my life.

I was a very young man of twenty-one years. And I was deeply in love.

The day was May 6, 1977. I asked my girlfriend, Nellie Jo, to marry me. I asked her to be my wife. And she gave me an incredible gift of grace.

She said "yes."

We would get married on December 17, 1977. And after nearly four decades, I still look back on that day in May in amazement. At times, I am dumbfounded by her response.

She said "yes."

You see, I can really be a jerk at times. I can let my temper get the best of me. I can be so busy doing good things that I neglect the best things. Like my family. Like my wife.

But, through it all, Nellie Jo has stood by me. She has loved me. She has forgiven me.

One time, in fear and trembling, I asked her. I asked her why she has remained so faithful and loving when I have been a lousy husband at times. Her response was incredibly simple, but incredibly revealing.

"Thomas," she began. She's the only person who calls me "Thomas." I like it. She continued, "When I said, 'I do' and 'for better or worse,' I meant it. I knew we would not always have easy times. I knew there would be struggles. But I made a commitment to you. I made my mind up. That has been my attitude from the first day of our marriage."

Stop for just a moment. Did you catch that last sentence?

"That has been my attitude from the first day of our marriage."

Nellie Jo made a decision. She made a decision about her attitude.

## Our Attitude about Our Church

This book is about what we should *do* in our church. But before we go further talking about *doing*, we must address the issue of our attitude.

If we do without the right attitude, we submit to legalistic guidelines. We become frustrated. We burn out.

But if we have the right attitude, doing becomes natural. It becomes joyous. In other words, if you have a right, biblically directed attitude, you will experience joy in church membership.

The right attitude means we recognize that no church is perfect. We expect that some church members will be irritants to us. We acknowledge that no pastor or church staff member is perfect.

But we serve and do anyway. We serve and do, not out of a sense of legalistic obligation, but out of an overflow of gratitude of what God has done for us through His Son.

So what exactly does the right attitude look like? Let's look at four biblical examples.

## The Right Attitude: *I Am a Unifying Church Member*

The health of any group is tied to its unity. It's true for sports teams. It's true for businesses. It's true for families. And it's true for churches.

But here is the thing about unity. It only works when individuals have made a decision. Each individual in the group must decide to put the good of the group before his or her own needs. It only works for individuals who have the right attitude.

Paul emphasized unity very clearly as he wrote to different churches. Read what he said to the church at Ephesus: "Therefore I, the prisoner for the Lord, urge you to walk worthy of the calling you have received, with all humility and gentleness, with patience, accepting one another in love, diligently keeping the unity of the Spirit with the peace that binds us" (Eph. 4:1–3).

Let's be clear. The Bible mandates us to have an attitude of unity in the church. But look at what it requires: humility, gentleness, patience, and acceptance of one another in love. Have you ever been to a church business meeting where some of those requirements were not met? Have you ever been to a church business meeting where none of those requirements were met? Have you ever been to a church business meeting where true humility is displayed?

Unity requires humility. That means we view others as better than ourselves.

Unity requires gentleness. That means we control our temper and demonstrate kindness to other church members, whether they are good guys or jerks.

Unity requires patience. That means we put up with a lot even if we are frustrated and perplexed at the behavior and attitude of others.

Unity requires acceptance of one another in love. That means we accept people unconditionally. It doesn't mean we condone sinful behavior. But it does mean we demonstrate a lot of grace.

Okay, I admit it. I just read my own words. I looked at the requirements of unity, and I thought, *No way!* There is no way I can be humble, gentle, patient, and loving to some of the people I know.

And then I remember.

I remember how much Christ loves me. I remember how He died for me. I remember how I deserve none of it.

It was grace. Totally unmerited favor. In His strength, I can have an attitude of unity. Indeed, I must have an attitude of unity.

## The Right Attitude: *I Am a Sacrificial Church Member*

If we have any doubt about this attitude, look at these words from Philippians 2:5–8:

> Make your own attitude that of Christ Jesus, who, existing in the form of God, did not consider equality with God as something to be used for His own advantage. Instead He emptied Himself by assuming the form of a slave, taking on the likeness of men. And when He had come as a man in His external form, He humbled Himself by becoming obedient to the point of death—even to death on a cross.

Read those words again slowly. We are to have the attitude of Christ, the sacrificial attitude that took Him to death on a cross.

I wish I had asked my dad a lot more questions before he died. I wish I had insisted he tell me more about his life.

I now want to hear more about how he sacrificed for his siblings when his mother died. He was only ten years old. His dad, an alcoholic, took to the bottle until his death.

I now want to hear more about how he sacrificed for his country. He was a top turret gunner on a B21 airplane in World War II. He was wounded and received the Purple Heart. He received other medals of valor.

I now want to hear more about how he sacrificed for his home, a small town in south Alabama. I want to hear about his years as a mayor where he guided the town in the turbulent 60s and 70s when race tensions were at a peak.

But Dad died when I was twenty-eight years old. I never asked him enough questions. I never listened enough to him tell his stories of courage and sacrifice.

You see, when we sacrifice, we are acting most like Christ. We are learning that the greatest joy comes when we put others before ourselves.

By the way, Paul wrote these words to church members in Philippi. They were written in the very clear context regarding the attitude of church members. They were to have an attitude of sacrifice. It was a clear and powerful mandate for church members 2,000 years ago.

And it still is for us today.

## The Right Attitude: *I Am a Prayerful Church Member*

Her name is Lillian. When I became the pastor of a church in St. Petersburg, Florida, I immediately noticed her attitude. It was obvious. She told me she would be praying for me and for my ministry every day. She meant it.

I have no doubt Lillian prayed for me. I have no doubt her prayers were a primary reason my ministry in St. Petersburg was so blessed.

The apostle Paul knew about the power of prayer in the church. These powerful words were written to the church at Colosse:

For this reason also, since the day we heard this, we haven't stopped praying for you. We are asking that you may be filled with the knowledge of His will in all wisdom and spiritual understanding, so that you may walk worthy of the Lord, fully pleasing to Him, bearing fruit in every good work and growing in the knowledge of God. (Col. 1:9–10)

Paul had an attitude of prayerfulness. And he wanted all the members of the church to have that attitude.

Let me remind you of this prayerful attitude in the context of 1 Timothy 3:7: "Furthermore, he must have a good reputation among outsiders, so that he does not fall into disgrace and the Devil's trap." This sentence is one of the qualifications of a pastor. He must have a good reputation among the outsiders, or the unbelievers, who are not a part of the church. Then the verse refers to "the Devil's trap."

The word *trap* is a rare usage in the Bible. Traps are never set unintentionally. It is a strategic and powerful threat by Satan to take down pastors and church leaders. It is a real threat, a powerful threat.

So how do we respond? The Bible is very clear that we fight this spiritual reality with our spiritual strength: prayer. Immediately after Paul tells the church to put on the full armor of God to fight spiritual warfare, he closes with an admonition of prayer: "Pray at all times in the Spirit with every prayer and request, and stay alert in this with all perseverance and intercession for all the saints" (Eph. 6:18).

There are all kinds of attitudes you can have in your church. One of those is an attitude of prayer.

## The Right Attitude: *I Am a Joyful Church Member*

Have you ever noticed that grateful people are joyous people? Paul gave the Philippian church a command to rejoice, and he tied the spirit of joy to an attitude of thanksgiving or gratitude:

> Rejoice in the Lord always. I will say it again: Rejoice! Let your graciousness be known to everyone. The Lord is near. Don't worry about anything, but in everything, through prayer and petition with thanksgiving, let your requests be made known to God. And the peace of God, which surpasses every thought, will guard your hearts and minds in Christ Jesus. (Phil. 4:4–7)

Paul shoots straight with us. If we are to really have joy in our lives, we must be gentle and gracious. We are to pray instead of worry. And as we pray, we are to pray with a spirit of thanksgiving or gratitude.

Have you ever seen a GCM? That's my acronym for a "grumpy church member." They are the church members most likely to complain at church business meetings. They are the persistent critics of the pastor and staff. They are the members who view the church as an organization where they pay their dues to get their perks and their privileges. And they are grumpy and divisive when they don't.

Contrast them to a JCM ("joyous church member"). A joyous church member counts her blessings. She is grateful for the freedom and opportunity to worship with other believers. She is a constant source of encouragement to pastors, church staff, and fellow church members.

The JCM is always grateful. The GCM is regularly complaining and frustrated. The JCM looks for opportunities to encourage and give. The GCM nitpicks and finds fault in many things.

That is why one member is joyful and another is grumpy. It's all a matter of attitude.

When we received the gift of salvation, we became a part of the body of Christ. Read how the Bible describes this gift: "Now you are the body of Christ, and individual members of it. And God has placed these in the church" (1 Cor. 12:27–28).

Did you get that? When you received the free gift of salvation, you also received the gift of membership into the body of Christ.

Membership in the body of Christ, the church, is a gift from God.

And when we receive a gift, we should be joyous and grateful.

It really is a matter of our attitude.

## Time to Move from "I Am" to "I Will"

Your attitude determines who you are: I am joyous. I am angry. I am grateful. I am jealous.

You get the picture. Our attitudes are the foundations of our actions. If I am joyous, I will tend to be an encouraging person. If I am angry, I will tend to be a critical person.

Let me return to the opening story in this chapter. This time let me talk about my marriage to Nellie Jo from my own perspective.

Let's presume I have all the healthy attitudes in place. I love her unconditionally. I focus on her strengths more than her weaknesses. I am grateful for her, for the gift from God that she is to me.

And that's it.

I never serve her. I never ask her out for a date. I never offer her words of encouragement. I rarely spend time with her.

So what would Nellie Jo think of my good attitudes? She would rightly think they are contrived and insincere. She would doubt my commitment. She would wonder if I am truly committed to our marriage.

Maybe many of you church members do indeed have a good attitude. Maybe you are not in the group that whines, complains, nags, and pouts. Maybe your heart is really in the right place.

So here is my simple question. Is your attitude reflected in your actions? In case you are wondering where I am headed with this question, let me offer you an example.

Several years ago, we considered the most active church members who attended church around three times a week. They might attend a Sunday morning Bible study or a Sunday morning worship service. Others might return for Sunday evening events or Wednesday activities.

Do you know how much that perspective has changed in just a few years? Today, many pundits define an active church member as someone who attends church events or services at least three times a month.

Did you get that? An active church member has now been re-defined from three times a week to three times a month!

I can anticipate potential objections, "Don't make this matter a legalistic obligation! We don't need an activity checklist to be close to God!"

I understand. But let me ask you this question. Would your spouse think you are still devoted to him or her if you decided to reduce your time with him or her by 75 percent? That's what is happening with even some of our most committed church members.

It's time. It's time for a decision. It's time for a church membership revolution. Not because we are legalistically obligated. Not because we equate activities to commitment. But because a great attitude toward your church, the bride of Christ, will result in great actions for her.

Will you join me in this revolution? Will you prayerfully consider giving your life's all in commitment to Christ through His church? Will you be a part of a movement that will change the world as the body of Christ unites in force with renewed effort and renewed zeal?

It's time. Christ is calling all church members to forsake self and to serve others for His sake. In doing so, our church becomes our priority and our focus as it was in the New Testament.

Listen carefully to this call of God. Listen to how you can discern your commitment in His church. And when you begin to understand the action plans He has set before you, be prepared to respond with two simple words.

I will.

## Points to Ponder

1. Explain how Ephesians 4:1–3 works in the context of our relationship with fellow church members.

2. Why do you think church members are less committed to their churches today than they were several years ago?

3. Read again Philippians 2:5–8. How does this passage relate to our commitment in our church today?

4. Would you say your commitment to your church is more or less today than it was five years ago? Why?

## Chapter 2

# I Will Worship with Others

**Y**ou had to admire his commitment.

He made the decision to attend. He would not miss it. The weather was terrible that day—steady rain, temperature in the forties. He still got out in the weather.

Because of the bad weather, he did not quite make it on time. It was difficult to get to his seat as well. But he persevered. His seat was not comfortable, but he neither left nor complained. His presence vividly demonstrated his love and commitment.

He was joyous the entire time. He enjoyed the presence of fellow believers. His attitude, his attendance, and his enthusiasm all reflected his deep and abiding commitment.

He was at a college football game on a Saturday afternoon.

By the way, he did not attend church worship services the next day. He was tired from the ball game. And there was a 40 percent chance of rain.

## With Others

True worship flows from the heart in recognition and response to the magnificence of Christ, and because of an understanding of the grace found solely in the gospel. Embracing these truths through the practical experience of daily living is imperative in our relationship with God.

And while true worship always manifests itself in the individual's response to the majesty of God, true biblical worship manifests itself in experience with other believers as well. We call that corporate worship. In the vernacular of some, we have called it "going to church."

I love reading the story of the early churches in the books of Acts and Paul's letters to various churches. Very soon after Peter preached his sermon at Pentecost in Acts 2, the Jerusalem church began gathering in corporate worship. This description in Acts 2:46–47 is one of my favorites:

> Every day they devoted themselves to meeting together in the temple complex, and broke bread from house to house. They ate their food with a joyful and humble attitude, praising God and having favor with all the people. And every day the Lord added to them those who were being saved.

Now that's "going to church"!

They *devoted themselves* to this practice. They did not gather together to check off some legalistic guideline. The word *devoted* means it was a motive of a passion, heart, and desire.

They were *joyful*. Because their focus was on God, they could only be joyful. They did not go for a worship experience. They went to experience God in worship

They had *humble attitudes*. That meant they put others before themselves. They were not there to complain that the music style was not their preference, that the sermon went too long, or that someone had their seat or pew. They were there in humility before God and others.

They had *favor with all the people*. "The people" refers to those outside the church, in other words, the unbelievers. And God used the joyful witness and attitudes of the believers for an incredible result: *And every day the Lord added to them those who were being saved* (Acts 2:47).

This biblical perspective of corporate worship is so different from how it's practiced in many of our churches. We should not "go to church" to get our self-centered needs met. Instead we go to worship the one true God as we serve alongside other believers.

## Meet the Archibalds

My dad desired to vacation in one place every summer when I was young: Panama City Beach, Florida. Every year we stayed in the same motel: the Bel Air. We stayed for the same length of time: two weeks. And we went the same month of the year: July.

Dad really knew how to take a vacation. He disconnected from work. He spent hours on the beach. He went deep-sea fishing. And he caught and cooked crabs.

Often, he would ask another family to join us for one or both weeks of the vacation. I have fond memories of spending time with numerous children from these families. One family I remember in particular was the Archibalds. Perhaps I remember them best because they interrupted Dad's routine.

You see, on a Saturday night, they told our family they would not be participating in our plans for the next morning. They were going to church.

*Wait a minute,* I thought. We were on vacation. That means vacation from everything, including church. And how could they go to church? They were three hours from our home church.

I would later learn how committed the Archibalds were to the local church. Even on those occasions when they were out of town, they found a church to attend. They did so joyously, not out of a sense of obligation.

My youthful memory also recalls that they did not try to heap guilt on our family for not joining them. This decision was theirs and theirs alone. We would have been welcome to join them, but they were not going to force the issue.

Let me pause for a moment to put this story in perspective. It took place fifty years ago, an entire half of a century. But to this day, I remember the Archibalds. I remember their joyous spirit. I remember their commitment. And I remember that Sunday they attended a church worship service.

## From Begrudging Participation to Joyous Commitment

In many of our churches, we have to beg people to attend worship services. But so many have inexcusable conflicts. Like the football game. Or the kid's soccer game. Or the traveling softball team. Or the weekend at the lake. Or the fact that I only slept five hours.

For many Christians, all other activities have become mandatory while the worship service has become an optional afterthought.

Jesus met a Samaritan woman at a well. You know the story. You know that Jesus knew her story. She was amazed. Do you remember the last words He spoke to her in John 4:23–24? "But an hour is coming, and is now here, when the true worshipers will worship the Father in spirit and truth. Yes, the Father wants such people to worship Him. God is spirit, and those who worship Him must worship in spirit and truth."

It is a stunning declaration of the commitment of worship. It is an incredible statement of God's own desire for us to worship Him.

Their worship of God would also manifest itself in corporate worship after Jesus ascended. It is a priority of God. It certainly should be one of our priorities.

When Paul wrote his letter to Philemon, he spoke of "the church that meets in your home" (Philem. 2). As the apostle did in his other letters, he wrote to a church of individual believers who came together to worship God. There is no hint that this practice was anything but a clear, expected, and joyous practice of believers.

Corporate worship is not one option among many. It should be a consistent and persistent practice of all believers. Like the people in the churches in the New Testament. Like the Archibalds. Like you.

I will worship with other believers.

## The Terrible Shift to the Preference Driven Church

I can't put a specific date on it. Smarter people than I have tried to explain it. Somewhere in the twentieth century, believers, particularly in America, began to shift from an attitude of self-sacrificing service to God and worship of God, to consumer-focused, self-serving attitudes.

It has been a terrible shift.

Some blame it on the secularization of our culture. Others point to the degradation of theology in our churches. Still others say local church leaders themselves have taken on corporate models and turned our churches into consumer-focused organizations.

There is probably some truth in all three explanations. But there is one thing we can say with certainty: the focus in too many of our church worship services is not on God. We are focused on our own selves, our own needs, and our own preferences. See if some of these comments from church members hit home. They come straight from my blog at ThomRainer.com.

*That music is not the style I'm accustomed to hearing. If they don't change things, I'm leaving this church.* Wars over worship styles have taken their toll on many of our congregations. Churches have split. Members have stop attending. Church business meetings have turned into verbal brawls. Pastors and worship leaders have been forced out of their jobs.

No, I'm not suggesting we shouldn't have our own preferences about worship and music styles. And we should certainly be given the freedom to provide input about those matters. But I know the lack of civility, the harsh words, and divided churches cannot be ascribed to worship. Those are sinful and self-serving behaviors.

*I don't like the pastor's preaching.* Okay, let me be clear here. You certainly should expect your pastor to preach the Word. But preference-driven church members have different agendas. They want the sermon to be their preferred length. They want their pastor to emulate the latest and most popular podcast preacher. Indeed, many church members would like to assign their own texts and topics to be preached each week. Their agenda is not about worshipping God when the Word of God is preached. To the contrary, their agenda is about themselves.

Their focus has turned from God to self. They are not worshipping God with fellow believers.

*I am not comfortable in the worship services.* "Someone is sitting in my pew." "The cushions on the chair are not comfortable." "I don't like the times of the services."

"The music is too loud." "We have to sit too close together."

You get the picture. The time of corporate worship is about me, myself, and I. It is about my needs, my preferences, and my wants. It's hard to find God in this scenario. It is all about us. It's not all about God.

## It's Time to Say "I Will" to Corporate Worship

One of the many variations of the definitions of *corporate* is: "pertaining to a united group assembled for a greater good." When we worship, we are focusing our hearts on God. When we are in corporate worship, we should be focusing our hearts on God alongside other believers. There is something powerful, even miraculous, about believers united together to worship God.

So what can we do to make certain we are truly committed to corporate worship? How can we turn the focus away from ourselves and toward God? Consider the following four simple items of action and accountability.

*I will attend worship services.* It's just that simple. It's amazing how we do something when it becomes our priority. Some of you may have neglected the priority of corporate worship. Anything and everything becomes an excuse not to attend. See what happens when sports, entertainment, and vacations have a lower priority than corporate worship. See what happens when you make a firm commitment to God that you will attend weekly worship services.

*I will pray before I attend worship services.* Sometimes I might pray the night before. On other occasions I might pray the morning of worship services. I will pray for my own attitude of worship. I will pray for God to speak to me in the worship services. I will pray for others who are in the worship services. I will pray for my family that we will not have conflicts and get frustrated before we attend.

*I will pray as I enter the worship center or sanctuary.* Once again I will pray for my own heart and attitude. Again, I will pray for fellow believers who are worshipping God with me. I will pray for unbelievers that they will hear the gospel clearly, and that God's Spirit will convict them of sin and the need for a Savior. Finally, I will pray for all distractions to be removed that I, as well as others, may be focused on the true worship of God.

*I will pray that I will be a worshipper instead of a judge.* Too many times we leave a corporate worship service as if we just judged an Olympic event. We might give the pastor a "7" for the sermon, or the worship leader a "6" for the music. And we might give other worshippers a low "3" because they would not move to the middle of the pews to let us in more easily.

When we leave with such judgmental perceptions, we have not worshipped God. Instead we have attended an event to entertain us. We must pray that we will worship God instead of judging aspects of the corporate worship services. We must pray for a focus on Him instead of a focus on others.

## The Corporate Worship Revolution

It's both a sad and amazing reality. Many of our congregations consider church members to be in good standing if they only attend twice a month, or once a month, or hardly ever. In just a few short decades, commitment levels to corporate worship have declined precipitously.

It is time for a corporate worship revolution. It's time to make that moment of gathered believers a priority in our lives. It's time to stop making worship attendance an optional activity.

It's time to ask God to get our hearts right so we desire to worship Him in a corporate setting, not because we have some legalistic obligation to do so. It's time to urge others in the congregation to make corporate worship a priority. It is truly time for a corporate worship revolution.

Will you join me and millions of others in this revolution? Will you make this time a priority in your life? May we shout our commitment with God-given zeal and sincerity.

I will worship with others.

## Points to Ponder

1. Reflect on the declining commitment to attend worship services over the past few decades. Why do you think this development has emerged?

2. What are some actions you and others can take immediately to have a greater commitment to corporate worship?

3. Read Acts 2:41–47. Why was the level of commitment so high among the believers in the early church?

4. Read John 4:21–24. What did Jesus mean by worshipping God "in spirit and in truth"?

## Chapter 3

# I Will Grow Together with Others

It had been thirty-two years since I left the church.

The church was Golden Springs Baptist Church in Anniston, Alabama. I was honored and humbled to preach at the congregation's 50th anniversary.

You see, the people of that church mean so much to me. They were instrumental in my call to vocational ministry. Indeed, my family and I would leave the world of corporate banking to move to seminary to answer that call.

I loved seeing so many people I loved, so many people who invested so much in me.

Among them was Steve.

What was somewhat humorous is the way Steve greeted me that day: "Do you remember the balcony?" he asked. Of course, I remembered the balcony. It was the only space left for a Sunday school class in that growing church. The men's class I taught had to meet in the balcony.

Good times.

But my point is not the balcony per se. It's the connection between me and Steve. After thirty-two years, we were still connected to one another because we were in a group together. We called it "Sunday school" then. Some still use that name. Others call it small groups, life groups, home groups, or dozens of other names.

The point is that Steve and I developed a lifelong relationship in a group. And though more than three decades had separated us, we still remembered the balcony where the group met.

## Church Groups Then, and Now

Let's go back further than thirty-two years ago. Let's go back 2,000 years to a time when the first Christian church in Jerusalem was formed. In the previous chapter we looked at this text in the context of corporate worship. Now let's see the church in the context of gathered groups in Acts 2:46: "Every day they devoted themselves to meeting together in the temple complex, and broke bread from house to house."

Note closely the two contexts where the early believers met. They gathered for worship in the temple courts, and then they gathered in groups in their homes. The health of the early church was intricately tied to both the larger meeting and the smaller meeting context. It was not either/or. It was both/and.

It has been a constant theme throughout most of the history of the church. Those in churches gathered in both larger and smaller groups. Of course, there were exceptions, such as when churches had to go underground to avoid persecution.

For the most part, however, smaller groups have been tied to the health of the church.

Fast-forward 2,000 years.

Several years ago, I had my own wake-up call about the power of groups when I was leading a research project. I would report the research in my book, *High Expectations*. I asked my research team to review the records of hundreds of church members who had joined their churches five years earlier. We then asked the staff of these churches to identify those members who attended worship services only, and those who were also in a group.

The results were staggering.

Those church members who became involved in some type of group in the churches were *five times* more likely to be active in the church five years later compared to the worship-only attenders. (We did not include those who moved to another community, became incapacitated, or died in the dropout category.)

I had to check the results a second time. They were astounding. More than 83 percent of those who joined and were involved in a small group were still active in the churches. But only 16 percent of those who attended worship services only remained in the churches five years later.

I have led a lot of research projects, and I have read even more. But these results were some of the most surprising and most amazing I have ever seen.

And it brings us back to the main theme of this chapter. We cannot grow effectively as a believer in isolation. While we certainly need to be in larger worship settings, we also need to be connected in groups in the church: small groups, Sunday school classes, life groups, home groups, or others.

Why? Why are groups so powerful in local churches? What is it about groups that increase assimilation by a factor of five? Four primary factors contribute to it.

## The Relationship Factor

Do you remember Steve from the first part of this chapter? He was the guy who mentioned the balcony to me. Do you know why I'm writing about Steve more than three decades later? We established a strong relationship because we were in the same group for three years.

We obviously saw each other every week, but it was more than that. Our group had fun fellowship times in each other's homes. We went to ballgames together. We served together in ministry and mission projects.

We connected. Because of our common group, we connected.

Now, I'm about to make some pretty bold statements about groups, the church, and you. Don't be offended. Just hear me out.

If you are not in a group, you are not really committed to your church. If you are not in a group, you are, at best, a marginal church member. If you are not in a group, the likelihood of your dropping out from your church is high.

If you are not in a group, you could be a Christian sluggard. That means you may be an incredibly lazy and uncommitted Christian.

It means you are unwilling to grow spiritually together with other Christians. And if you think Lone Ranger Christianity is acceptable to God, you need to read the New Testament again. It's time for millions of church members to connect relationally by getting involved in a group.

## The Ministry Factor

One of the reasons I was so close to many of the young men in my small group at the Golden Springs Baptist Church is that we did ministry and missions together.

It was an expectation in our church that every adult group act as a church within the church in many ways. So we took care of one another. After my wife, Nellie Jo, came home from the hospital with each of our sons, someone from my group would be there with food and prayer.

We would not let anyone go in need. I remember when George lost his job, the men in his group chipped in to provide financial support for him and his family. And I will never forget the family our group "adopted," a single mom with five kids. She had been abused and then abandoned by her husband. We men and our wives became a second family to her. Our group ministered to her for two years until she remarried and got back on her feet.

Those are just a few of my stories. And those stories have been, and will be, mirrored millions of times by church members across the world. The body of Christ functions more like the body because so much ministry is taking place in groups.

Simply stated, ministry is more likely to take place with people who know each other well. And the primary way we can know other church members well is to be in a group together.

## The Teaching Factor

Learning the truths about Scripture can take place in different venues, but there are three venues that have been consistent throughout much of the history of the church. Of course, the preaching of the Word is paramount. Paul spoke of the primacy of preaching numerous times. For example, he wrote to the church at Corinth, "When I came to Troas to preach the gospel of Christ, the Lord opened a door for me" (2 Cor. 2:12).

When we sit under the preaching of the Word, we are learning the truths of Scripture taught by a preacher. It is one of the key facets of corporate worship.

We also learn the Bible by our own personal study. My personal practice is to read the Bible daily, going through the entire Bible each year. I read portions of the Old Testament, New Testament, Psalms, and Proverbs every day. I am always amazed how much new I learn every day by this practice I have done for years. I love studying God's Word.

The third most common venue is to learn the Bible in a smaller group within the church. Some of the most powerful and poignant teaching moments can come as you interact with others who are studying the same passage. The passage in Proverbs 27:17 certainly applies to those who interact in a group setting: "Iron sharpens iron, and one man sharpens another."

Jim is my all-time favorite Bible study teacher in a group setting. He would patiently listen to each of us young men many years ago as we attempted to tackle passage after passage. Looking back, I realize how far-fetched some of our discussions were, mine included. But Jim never spoke condescendingly to us. He never made us feel badly for our biblical excursions.

Jim asked questions. Good questions. Questions that made us think.

And so we let the "iron sharpen iron." We learned from each other. We encouraged each other. We challenged each other.

We did so because we were in a group. Groups matter.

## The Evangelism Factor

Not all groups are evangelistic. But any group can be evangelistic. Let me illustrate.

Roger is an introvert. I understand fully. So am I.

Roger knew he was commanded in Scripture to share the gospel with others. And he knew his introversion was no excuse to be disobedient.

He felt shame when he would go to lunch with Gene who could begin a conversation with almost anyone. He would listen and watch as Gene began a conversation with a server. He was amazed how easily Gene moved to a conversation about the gospel. He could do it almost every time,

So Roger tried. He tried with difficulty. He tried unsuccessfully. And he felt terrible about his efforts.

He quit trying.

One day Roger was talking to his neighbor, Ethan. He knew Ethan was not a Christian. In fact, his neighbor had told Roger bluntly that he didn't believe Jesus was the Son of God.

So Roger approached Ethan differently. He simply said to his neighbor, "Ethan, I don't want to force you into a conversation that would make both of us uncomfortable. Let me ask you this. Would you be willing to come to my Bible study group for a couple of weeks? The guys there are great. You know many of them. If you don't like it, you don't have to keep attending."

Much to Roger's surprise, Ethan showed up the next week. And the next week. And the next.

Much to Roger's surprise, Ethan started attending worship services. He brought his wife and two daughters.

Much to Roger's surprise, Ethan professed Christ and joined the church. His wife did as well. His two teenage daughters did as well.

Yes, Roger is an introvert. But he can invite someone to his Bible study group. He was amazed. Four people became believers in Christ. It began when Ethan started attending a group. Groups matter.

## Why Groups Matter

We could spend the entirety of this book talking about the importance of groups. For now, let's focus on four major issues related to groups.

*First, the health of the church is directly tied to the health of groups in the church.* If you are not in a small group, a Sunday school class, or some other type of group, you are not contributing to the health of the church. Indeed, you are not doing all you should be doing for your own spiritual health. Though we grow spiritually in our own personal devotional time, we also grow in community with others. A healthy church will inevitably have a large percentage of its worship attendance in groups.

*Second, groups in the church help close the back door.* Don't let this escape your notice. Someone who is in a small group in the church is five times more likely to remain active in the church than someone who is only attending worship services.

Think of the implications of this statistic. That person in a small group is five times more likely to be in ministry. Five times more likely to share their faith. Five times more likely to have a deeper knowledge of the Bible. Five times more likely to hear the gospel.

So, the issue is not simply about closing the back door. It's about believers having a deeper walk with Christ. It's about churches becoming healthier as a result.

It's about the power of groups.

*Third, you as a church member should be committed to being a part of a small group in your church.* Let me be clear. If you are not in a small group or Sunday school class, you are not fully committed to your church. You are a marginal or peripheral member. You may be in the larger gathering of corporate worship, but you are not in community.

And don't forget, if you are not in a group in your church, you are more likely to become disenchanted with your church. You are more likely to become a critic instead of an encourager. You are more likely to dropout of your church.

*Fourth, everyone in a group should be inviting others to the group.* It seems like it's not getting much attention these days. But inviting others to a group is one of the most effective ways to reach people and to assimilate them. Group outreach addresses the issue of growth and assimilation.

It's simple but profound. Groups are critically important to the church. And church members must be in groups to be truly committed.

## A Word to Church Leaders

Okay, before we leave this chapter, I want to have a brief word with you church leaders. My conversation to this point has been with church members in general.

Church leader, my question is simple. I hope it's profound. Are you leading your church or your area of ministry toward a greater awareness and emphasis on groups? Are you one of the biggest cheerleaders and encouragers for small groups, life groups, Sunday school classes, or whatever names your groups have?

You have read in this chapter about the importance of groups. If you are neglecting being a leader for groups in your church, you are not contributing to the well-being of your church.

Church leaders and church members, please hear me clearly. Groups matter.

And the next time you have the opportunity to join a group or lead a group more effectively, prayerfully consider one simple response.

I will.

## *Points to Ponder*

1.  Read Acts 2:41–47. Discuss how groups were one of the important facets of healthy church life in the Jerusalem church.

2.  Discuss four reasons why groups are so important in the church.

3.  What are three ways we learn Scripture more effectively? How is Scripture learning unique in groups?

4.  Give some common excuses why some church members are not in a group. What are your responses to these excuses?

# Chapter 4

# I Will Serve

**D**o you remember Heather from the introduction? She is the single mom of three kids. She recently joined The Church at Fountain Hill after several years' absence from being involved in a local church.

While the divorce from her husband precipitated her departure from Resurrection Community Church, there was another major factor at work. Stated simply, she had become sick of being a self-serving Christian. While she did not notice her attitude at Resurrection Community Church, she definitely noticed the positive difference since she became a member of The Church at Fountain Hill.

The people were different at the new church. No, it wasn't a perfect church, but it was a place of joy and serving. Better yet, she thought, it was a joyous church *because* the members were serving.

Heather recently articulated her thoughts to her neighbor and friend, Rachel. "You know, Rachel," she began, "I've been trying to figure out the difference between the two churches. When I was at Resurrection Community, it was like eating dessert all the time. You enjoy it for a while, then you eat too much of it and get sick. You long for 'real' food."

She continued, "Because I was a part of the 'in' group at Resurrection Community, I learned how to expect and demand things. Church was all about me, myself, and I. Frankly, I just got sick of being so self-serving."

The change in Heather was noticeable to herself and to others. "I just find so much joy in serving others," she said. "That's how most of the members are at my church now. We don't serve in ministry because of some legalistic guidelines. We serve because we are motivated by joy to do so."

Heather used to dread going to church on Sundays. Now she wakes up with anticipation about attending. And she is involved in a small group and at least one short-term ministry each year. She serves in areas that energize her, not in areas where someone has given her a guilt trip to participate.

Indeed, the membership as a whole is like that at The Church at Fountain Hill. They are sacrificial. They are serving. And more times than not, they say "I will" to ministry opportunities.

## What Would Jesus Do?

A quick reading of the New Testament will give you an easy answer to that question. The scene is Jesus with His disciples. The mother of James and John, identified in the text as "the mother of Zebedee's sons," addresses Jesus. She speaks boldly to Him: "Promise that these two sons of mine may sit, one on

Your right and the other on Your left, in Your kingdom" (Matt. 20:21).

Jesus quickly tells her that she has no idea what she's talking about. Then the other ten disciples become indignant at James and John. It's a fight ready to happen.

But Jesus calls a time-out. The text literally says, "He called them over" (Matt. 20:25).

Now read carefully Jesus' response to all twelve disciples. It is powerful.

He began, "You know that the rulers of the Gentiles dominate them, and the men of high position exercise power over them. It must not be like that among you. On the contrary, whoever wants to become great among you must be your slave; just as the Son of Man did not come to be served, but to serve, and to give His life—a ransom for many" (Matt. 20:25–28).

Did you get that? Did you understand the full import of Jesus' words?

May I put the essence of these words in a modern vernacular for church members today? I hope you won't be too offended.

"Hey church members: I know that the world says put yourself first. Look after number one. But that's not the way you are supposed to do it. Stop complaining about the music style and what *you* want. Stop demanding church leaders to do things the way *you* would like them to be. Stop trying to get *your* way in church business meetings. Instead, put others first. Put your desires last. Become a servant instead of a whiner and complainer."

Jesus then offers Himself as an example for serving. Instead of coming to Earth as a political king, Jesus came to serve. Indeed His service would go all the way to the cross. He became sin. He took on our sin. He was crucified on that bloody cross of His own volition. He served you and me by dying for us.

We church members must cease and desist becoming "I want" members and become "I will" members.

We must serve instead of demanding our way.

That's what Jesus said. And that's what Jesus would do.

Paul specialized in selflessness. I would love for him to come to one of our rancorous church meetings and have a few words. I don't think he would be shy about addressing self-serving motives and actions.

Philippians is my favorite letter he wrote to a church. Note that some form of the word *joy* appears in the brief letter fourteen times. It is indeed the letter of joy.

And what was Paul doing to experience such joy? He was in prison. He was facing death. He was concerned about the churches. And, in the midst of it all, he was joyous.

The apostle explains the basis for his joy. Indeed in Philippians 2:5–11, he tells us that true joy comes from having an attitude like Jesus. And lest we doubt the meaning of Jesus' attitude, Paul says that the attitude took Him to "becoming obedient to the point of death—even to death on a cross" (Phil. 2:8).

It is with that context that Paul explains how we are to respond to one another in our churches: "Do nothing out of rivalry or conceit, but in humility consider others as more important than yourselves. Everyone should look out not only for his own interests, but also for the interests of others" (Phil. 2:3–4).

Paul made it clear.

Jesus made it clear.

We are to serve. That is the basis for joy. And that is what church members should do.

## The Serving Revolution

What if you were to suggest to your pastor that your church perform an experiment? Let's call it a ninety-day test. Ask for commitments from members who are willing to participate. During the ninety days, they are to ask nothing from the church. They are not to complain in any way.

In addition, they will commit two hours a week to serving someone else. They might write encouraging letters to other members. They might visit and serve the homebound. They might work in a local missions house. They might clean the church or work in the landscaping around the church facilities. They might pick up trash in the community. They might get involved in a prayer ministry. They might work in the church nursery or preschool.

That's it. For ninety days church members will commit to serve and to be other-focused. They will withhold negativity and complaining.

Obviously no church will get 100 percent commitments. But let's suppose your church gets 100 people to commit for ninety days. The church would have 100 people who refrain from negativity and complaining. The church would have members serving others for 2,600 hours over the ninety-day period.

It would be a revolution, a serving revolution. And I would anticipate that so much joy and excitement would be unleashed that your church would not want to return to "normal." Indeed, the serving revolution would become the new normal. Your church would become a greater functioning biblical church.

Now let's expand it a bit. Think about your church having a one-year serving challenge. Let's say your church had about 500 in attendance, and about 350 members make a commitment to serve one hour a week for an entire year.

Pause for a moment, and think of the implications. The commitment would be minimal: just one hour a week. But 350 members make the commitment for the entire church to be serving 350 hours a week for a year. That is a total of 18,200 hours. Or to put it another way, that would be like someone serving 455 weeks or almost nine years at forty hours a week.

The church would have a revolution, a serving revolution.

## Serving through Small Groups

I hope you heard my excitement for small groups in the previous chapter. Even more, I hope you saw the incredible power of small groups in action. Now, put small groups and serving ministry together and you have an absolutely powerful ministry.

Are you in a small group? A Sunday school class? A home group? Any kind of a group? When your group begins to serve in a prayerful and organized way, the impact is even more powerful.

I know of one group that "adopted" three struggling families with single moms. I know of another group that adopted the entire third grade of a lower-income public school and provided ministry, supplies, and childcare to the teachers, the students, and the students' families.

And then there is the Sunday school class that took on the trash pick-up project in their small town for an entire year. On almost any given week, you would see one or more of the class members picking up trash alongside the road.

The needs are endless. That means the opportunity for service is endless. We have come to expect the government to take on most of the social responsibilities in our culture today. What if churches and small groups had a service revolution? What would be the impact on both our culture and our churches?

## From "I Want" to "I Will Serve" in a Church That's Not Serving

I mentioned my blog earlier. At ThomRainer.com I have the honor of interacting with pastors, church staff, and lay leaders. Indeed, in the course of a year I will interact with over seven million viewers who offer more than ten thousand comments.

I get to hear from a lot of leaders. Most of them are incredibly gracious. Most of them are kind even when they offer constructive criticism. One of the more frequent types of comments or questions comes from those who are in churches like Resurrection Community Church. Many members in that church are self-serving. They are argumentative. They like to get their way. They treat the church like a country club: "I've paid my dues, so serve me."

The question to me is phrased something like this: "How can I be a healthy, serving church member in a church where the members are overall inwardly focused on themselves?"

My response is twofold. First, there are times when we should leave a church. As a rule, I am not a fan of "church hopping." But most church hopping takes place when a person is not getting his or her way in a church. In other words, the motive to leave is self-serving instead of serving. If our motive is to be in a place where you can joyously serve, maybe a move is in order.

The second response is preferable. Stay where you are and become an example of a serving Christian. One woman shared with me how her entire attitude changed when she started taking some intentional steps to serve. First, she made a commitment to stop being a critic or judge of everything that takes place in the church. Second, her daily prayer time included a petition to God that she might have an attitude of servanthood every day. Third, her prayer time each day also included prayers for specific leaders and members in the church, including those that irritated her. Fourth, she committed to a minimum of one hour of service through the church every week.

She wrote me a follow-up e-mail seven months after she made this commitment. Here is a portion of her comments:

"Thom, I have never been more joyful to be a church member! I don't have to worry about getting my way. My mission is now to serve others. It's much more fun to serve than to be served. I still pray every day for my attitude. And I pray for specific people in the church every day. That has changed my attitude incredibly.

"I have also made certain I do something of service in the church at least one hour a week. I volunteered for nursery duty once a month at the church. Then I committed to the shut-in ministry to visit at least three persons a month."

She concluded with these words:

"I truly have learned in action what Jesus meant when he said we would be first if we put ourselves last. I am last in the sense that I serve others before me. I am first in the sense that I have incredible joy coming directly from Jesus."

Her final two sentences were powerful and poignant:

"I wish I had made this effort years ago. I have truly learned how to experience the joy of Christ by serving."

## It Is Time

There has been a slow but discernible change in many of our churches. We have retreated into a self-serving shell and made church mostly about us.

It is time for a change.

It is time for a change that won't come from a denominational bureaucracy or a plug-and-play program.

It is time for church members to stop nitpicking the small issues in the church and to discover the needs and hurts where we can serve.

It is time for a change among church members around the world to seek to serve rather than seek to be served.

It will be a revolution! Will you join it?

If so, consider this commitment prayerfully and with total sincerity:

I will serve.

## *Points to Ponder*

1. Why do you think so many churches have become self-serving, like Resurrection Community Church, rather than other-serving, like The Church at Fountain Hill?

2. Read Matthew 20:20–28. What was the motive of the mother of Zebedee's sons in her request to Jesus? How does this passage relate to service in congregations today?

3. How could Philippians 2:1–18 relate to serving in the church today? Make certain you address verse 14 specifically.

4. Review again the story of Heather in this chapter and in the introductory chapter. What are some key lessons from her for church members today? Also, what are some specific ways you can be a greater servant in your church today?

# Chapter 5

# I Will Go

Only the name of the church has been changed. The facts have not.

Twin Springs Church started as a mission of a large downtown church. In the 1950s the population was moving toward the Twin Springs area. Some visionary leaders of the downtown church saw the possibilities of reaching more people with a new church in the growing community. So the church gave selflessly of people and money and time.

In 1955 a new church was born.

The early history of Twin Springs Church seems to be mostly positive. The church grew steadily from a core group of seven families to a peak of 450 in average worship attendance. The peak attendance occurred in 1985.

Hardly anyone noticed the decline. At least hardly anyone said anything about the decline. For the next three decades attendance declined steadily. But the decline was imperceptible to most of the members.

Let's put it in perspective. The decline average was only about one attendee each month. But in more than thirty years the decline in attendance was 360 in average attendance.

Did you get that? The decline was 360 in average attendance! The once vibrant church of 450 in attendance now only has ninety showing up on a typical Sunday.

What happened? Good question.

## The Diagnosis

My involvement was minimal, but the analysis was pretty simple. I compared the growth of the church with the growth of the community. The community was growing rapidly through 1985. The church benefitted from the demographic growth of Twin Springs, though its growth was not nearly as rapid as that of the community.

It was indeed simple. As the community grew, the church grew. The members and leaders of the church hardly had any intentional outreach or evangelism to the community. Twin Springs Church basically let people know the doors were open and they came.

At least they came until 1985.

The church probably would have grown as rapidly as the community had it been intentional about "going." But the leaders and members were content with a "y'all come" attitude. (Yes, the church is in the South.)

The church never developed a DNA of going. They rarely reached out beyond their own walls. The members became more inwardly focused. They focused more and more on their comfort and needs. The decline was inevitable and tragic.

Today the church of ninety in attendance is in a large facility it cannot afford. It has been twelve years since Twin Springs Church had a full-time pastor. Cash reserves are totally depleted.

I've seen it happen too many times. The church will close its doors in just a few years unless something dramatic and drastic takes place.

## The Story Is about You

I know. This story seems be about a church's decline. While that is part of the story, it's not the main issue. The key issue is about those who were and are in the church. It's not an institutional story. It's about me. And it's about you.

You see, Twin Springs Church was once full of members who made a decision to let their church be about them. Few members invited people to church. Even fewer shared the gospel with others in the community.

Twin Springs Church was about me, myself, and I.

When a church declines, we often want to blame the pastor. Or the church staff. Or other church members. Or the denomination. Or circumstances.

The reality is that church decline is the collective result of individuals who have decided they will not "go." The church thus becomes a religious country club instead of an obedient Great Commission congregation.

## The Story Is about Your Jerusalem

I know you are familiar with Acts 1:8. It is a post-resurrection narrative about Jesus right before He ascends to heaven. He leaves these last words with His followers: "But you will receive power when the Holy Spirit has come on you, and you will be My witnesses in Jerusalem, in all Judea and Samaria, and to the ends of the earth."

That was it. Those were Jesus' last words on Earth before He ascended. They are obviously important words. They came from Jesus. And they are His final words.

We could spend an entire book on the verse, but let's focus on the word *Jerusalem* for now. I don't want to minimize missions and evangelism beyond our communities, the "Judea, Samaria, and ends of the earth" part of the passage. I simply want us to discuss Jerusalem.

Why? Jerusalem, of course, is the immediate community of the church. And in many of our churches, it is the most neglected part of our mission field. In fact, in a study I led several years ago, our team found that fewer than 10 percent of the churches in the United States are growing at least at the pace of the community. Stated simply, most of our churches are losing ground in our communities.

We are not going.

## Our Belief Response

What, then, is our response? Allow me to address three major categories: our belief response, our objections, and our actions.

No believer or church member will feel compelled to share his or her faith if they don't really believe others need the gospel. Let me offer an extreme but, hopefully, clarifying illustration.

Suppose you see someone walking on a dry lake bed. There was once water there, but it's just dry, hard, and dusty now. Would you try to save them from drowning by diving in that dirt? Of course not. You know that they are not drowning, so they don't need saving.

We need to settle this issue first and foremost. Do you really believe those who are not Christians need saving? Do you really believe that those without Christ are lost? That is why Luke 19:10 makes it abundantly clear: "For the Son of Man has come to seek and to save the lost."

I fear that some of our church members only give lip service to the doctrine of lostness and to the belief that Christ is the only way of salvation. If we have no deep down belief in those truths, we will have no urgency to go.

Remember, Jesus Himself left no doubt about this issue. Jesus was speaking to His disciples in John 14:1–6 about eternal life when He said: "Your heart must not be troubled. Believe in God; believe also in Me. In My Father's house are many dwelling places; if not, I would have told you. If I go away and prepare a place for you, I will come back and receive you to

Myself, so that where I am you may be also. You know the way to where I am going."

Not Thomas. He had his doubts. He had uncertainties about this "way." And he does not hesitate to say so. "Lord," Thomas said, "we don't know where You're going. How can we know the way?"

Then it comes. Those words from Jesus that leave no doubt. Those words from Jesus that are pointed and powerful. "Jesus told him, 'I am the way, the truth, and the life. No one comes to the Father except through Me.'"

There you have it. The words are straight from Jesus Himself. The words are the gospel, the good news. There is a way. But it is the only way.

Do you really believe that?

Do you really believe that Christ is the only way of salvation? Do your actions reflect your beliefs? Are you constantly and urgently going and sharing your faith in words and deed?

## Our Response to Objections

You encounter that friend or that person at work. You think about inviting her to church, or starting a conversation about spiritual matters, or giving her a Bible as a gift. But you never move forward. Why?

You have begun to rationalize. You are giving yourself objections to your conviction to go. Thus you never broach the subject with her. You never invite her to church.

There are a number of objections we offer ourselves. They best fit in the category of excuses.

*That is not my spiritual gift.* Really? You think you are not spiritually gifted in evangelism, so you decide you can leave that responsibility to others. Think about the logical inconsistency of that objection. Would you say that those who do not have the gift of mercy should never show mercy? Of course not. Do you think that a person who does not have the gift of giving should never give? Everyone is called to be obedient to the Great Commission. Including me. And you.

*That is what we pay our pastor and church staff to do.* I use to think this objection was more of an attitude than a specifically articulated issue. But when I started doing church consultation, I heard it several times. I challenged one church member to show me in Scripture where evangelism and going was limited to the pastor. His response: "That's common sense. Everyone knows that's why you pay a pastor."

*I don't have time.* If we don't have time to share the love of Christ, it's really not a priority in our lives. It's a simple question: Is there anything more important than someone having a relationship with Jesus as Lord and Savior? If nothing is more important, how can we not have time to do it?

*I don't want to impose my beliefs on others.* This one is really bothersome. Can you imagine the apostle Paul standing before a crowd and saying, "I really have some good news for you, but I don't want to impose my beliefs on you. I'll just keep my beliefs to myself. After all, religion is really a private matter"? Of course not! The gospel is to be shared boldly and joyfully.

*I am an introvert.* Let me confess something to you. I used to get really mad at myself when I went somewhere with an extroverted Christian friend and listened to him share his faith. He could develop a conversation naturally and, before I knew it, he was saying something about Jesus. I am an introvert, and my personality did not lend itself naturally to that type of evangelism. So I started praying for other opportunities to share the gospel many years ago. It has been incredible to see how God opens doors for me when I simply ask him for opportunities. And those opportunities fit my introverted personality. Introversion is not a valid excuse.

## Our Response with Actions

So how do we go? How do we become that kind of church member who makes a difference in our Jerusalem?

Let's first go back to the issue of belief and motivation. Do you really believe that Christ is the only way of salvation? Are you then more motivated to share the gospel than anything else?

Look at two men who were indeed highly motivated. About 2,000 years ago, Peter and John were in prison. Their crime? They had been telling people about Jesus.

These two rabble-rousers appeared next before Jewish leadership to present their case. After hearing them, the leaders made a decision. They would let Peter and John go free if they would just keep their mouths shut about Jesus.

So what was their response? Here are their words directly from Acts 4:19–20: "Whether it's right in the sight of God for us to listen to you rather than to God, you decide, for we are unable to stop speaking about what we have seen and heard."

Did you get that? They were *unable* to stop speaking about Jesus. They couldn't stop speaking then, but many Christians today won't start speaking.

So let's go from theory to action. What are you to do? Specifically in the context of your church trying to reach your community, how do you get serious about reaching Jerusalem? Let me offer some concrete action steps.

*Pray for opportunities.* It's so simple, but it is rarely a step taken by church members. Before you go to bed tonight, pray that God will give you opportunities to share the love of Christ in word or deed. It is absolutely amazing how God responds.

I have many stories, but one of my favorites was after I prayed the simple prayer that morning for God to give me opportunities to share my faith. Before the afternoon was over, I got a call from a former boss (I was a banker before I became a vocational minister). He wanted to get together with me. I would soon find out that he sought me out because he had questions about Jesus.

Wow.

And here's another amazing part of the story. I had not heard from him for twenty-seven years! But the day I prayed for an opportunity, the call came.

Pray for opportunities.

*Invite people to church.* Again, this concept is so incredibly simple. When you invite someone to church, you are bringing him or her into fellowship with Christians. When you invite someone to church, he or she may have the opportunity to hear the gospel. I have seen the simple act of inviting have profound and eternal impact on entire families.

So, will people really come to church if we invite them? My research team and I did such a study several years ago. The results surprised all of us on the team. Eight out of ten people who do not attend church will come to church if someone invites them. That one statistic may be one of the most amazing we have uncovered in my twenty-five years of research.

If you invite them, they will come.

*Intentionally look for opportunities.* You are shopping for a car. The old faithful you have driven for fifteen years is no longer faithful. The repairs are more costly than the value of the car. You decide what your next car will be. Have you noticed what happens next? You begin to see that same model all over the place. You had not noticed it until now. Your framework had changed.

The same framework should take place with us spiritually. We should be viewing people and opportunities through the lens of evangelism. Because we are spiritually alert to such opportunities, we will see them more frequently.

*Be prepared to speak when the opportunity to arises.* You need to know what to say at that divine appointment. I have participated in many evangelism training programs, and they have all helped me to share my faith more cogently and consistently. One of my favorites today is "Three Circles." You can download the free app, "Life Conversation Guide." It is very simple and very helpful.

## It's Time to Go

If you are a typical church member, you may not do much to share the love of Christ with your community, your neighbors, your friends, or even your family. I think one of Satan's greatest tactics is to convince Christians they can be comfortably silent. It is a sin to be silent when we have been commanded to speak.

One person in one church can make a difference. One member committed to going can be a spark that ignites a fire.

One person.

You.

It is time for all church members and believers to acclaim these words without hesitation:

I will go.

### *Points to Ponder*

1.  Why do you think the typical church member does not invest time in "going" in their communities?

2.  Read Acts 4:1–22. How can that text have real-life application in the world today?

3.  How can you make your prayer life an instrument toward "going"?

4.  Do most church members act like they really believe John 14:1–6? Why or why not?

## Chapter 6

# I Will Give Generously

I wish you could have known Jess Keller. He was my uncle. He became a second dad to me when my own father died at a relatively young age.

Jess died a few years ago. I officiated at the funeral. The church was packed, somewhat unusual when people die in their older years. What took place after the funeral was even more amazing.

Person after person wanted to speak with me. No, they weren't really interested in me; they wanted me to hear their own story about Jess.

You see, in my funeral message, I mentioned Jess's generosity. When I was a struggling seminary student with a family of five, Uncle Jess sent money to us on five different occasions over a six-year period. I knew he was a man of prayer because the funds came at critical times for us. One of those occasions was when my wife had decided to sell her blood for money. Then came the check from Uncle Jess.

I knew Jess had been in prayer because he had no way of knowing how serious our financial distress was. He said in a letter to me: "God convicted me in prayer to send you these funds."

But let me return to the scene shortly after his funeral. So many people wanted me to know that Jess had done something similar for them. Not only were their stories amazing, the sheer numbers of people telling me the stories were incredible.

I would also hear affirmations of his generosity to his church. He was serious about giving beyond a tithe.

One man summed it well: "Jess Keller was the most generous person I have ever known. And he seemed to take great joy in giving."

Those two sentences were powerful. He not only was generous. He found great joy in giving.

By the way, when my third son was born, Nellie Jo and I had no doubt what his name would be. We named him Jess.

## The Greatest Sermon Ever

The crowds surrounded Jesus. They all wanted to hear from Him. So He went up on a mountain and began to speak. You will never hear a more powerful sermon. It is commonly known as the Sermon on the Mount.

Volumes have been written on this sermon. He amazed the audience with His words. We still are amazed today. Indeed, anytime I read this sermon from Matthew 5 to 7, I come away with renewed conviction and renewed zeal. Such was the reaction of the crowds who had the rare opportunity to hear it in person: "When Jesus had finished the sermon, the crowds were astonished at His teaching, because He was teaching them like one who had authority, and not like their scribes" (Matt. 7:28–29).

The subjects Jesus covers are pointed and convicting. Near the halfway mark of the Sermon on the Mount, He begins to talk about money. You can almost imagine the discomfort of the crowd. Perhaps many look down or shuffle their feet.

Jesus says, "Don't collect for yourselves treasures on earth, where moth and rust destroy and where thieves break in and steal. But collect for yourselves treasures in heaven where neither moth nor rust destroys, and where thieves don't break in and steal. For where your treasure is, there your heart will be also" (Matt. 6:19–21).

Stunning words. Amazing words. For both a first-century audience and a twenty-first century audience.

Jesus says we are not to focus on collecting material wealth. No, He is not advocating that we don't save money; He is focusing on the heart issue of money. If we are not to "collect," then the obvious corollary is that we are to give.

And as we give, we are actually collecting treasures in heaven. Simply stated, our giving has positive and eternal consequences. But if we don't give, our possessions have no value. They are subject to erosion or theft. They could be gone in an instant.

Then Jesus offers the most powerful punch of this portion of the message: "For where your treasure is, there your heart will be also" (Matt. 6:21).

Ouch.

You've probably heard a preacher say the corny line, "You can tell more about a person from his checkbook than anything else." You may cringe when you hear it. It's a line that had been repeated countless times.

But there is something we should know about that corny line: It is right. Where our money goes is a reflection of our heart and our priorities. Perhaps we should render a more modern contextualization to the corny sentence: "You can tell more about a person from his checkbook and digital debit card transactions than anything else."

Jesus, however, does not stop there. He says you will either have Him as your Lord or money as your lord. If you are obsessed with your money, He is not your Lord. If you focus on your money instead of Jesus, He is not your Lord. If you are not generous with your money, He is not your Lord.

Get the picture?

Jesus told the crowd on the mountainside these powerful words: "No one can be a slave of two masters, since he will hate one and love the other, or be devoted to one and despise the other. You cannot be slaves of God and of money" (Matt. 6:24).

We sometimes want to tiptoe through this issue of money. Maybe we are uncomfortable with the topic. Maybe we are uncomfortable with sermons and lessons on the topic. But it is an issue of great magnitude, an issue of the heart. Jesus said it was so.

It's really very simple. If we are not cheerfully generous with the funds God has entrusted to us, we are not an obedient follower of Christ. We have made a very clear statement that our heart is not with Christ. For where our treasure is, so will our heart also be.

## The Shift in Local Congregations

I can't pinpoint an exact date, but it began somewhere in the 1970s and 1980s. Money and stewardship became a delicate, if not taboo, topic in many churches. The possible reasons are many.

Some church leaders feared that mentioning money in worship services would drive away guests. Perhaps they were responding to legalistic demands for giving from the congregation. Or perhaps they simply overreacted. So the topic of stewardship was rarely broached for a season.

A number of critics focused on the extravagant lifestyles of a few ministers, particularly some that had a television or radio ministry. Though those preachers were a distinct minority, they were highly visible. They became a convenient excuse for people not to give.

It seems, though, the greatest shift took place in the attitudes of a number of church members. Have you ever heard of a church member withholding his or her funds because he or she does not like something in the church? Or perhaps even more pervasive are church members whose giving is calibrated by their precise definition of what the church should be doing.

I understand that church members should provide guidance on how church funds are spent. I understand that a few churches do abuse the common sense guidelines of transparency and accountability. But they are only a small number of the total congregations.

The reality is that many church members have developed a consumer mind-set on giving to local churches. If the church does not do things exactly as they want, they will withhold funds or reduce their giving.

No church will satisfy you 100 percent with their use of funds. But make certain you are in a church where you can give cheerfully, even when you don't agree with everything. We cannot think of the funds we give as "our" funds. The act of giving is the act of letting go. Such is the definition of a gift.

That was the attitude of my Uncle Jess. He gave to people and to organizations abundantly and cheerfully. And his church was his first priority. One person after his funeral said to me, "I bet he also gave a tithe to this church," as she reflected on his other gifts to people and organizations. A deacon from the church interjected with a smile, "Oh, Jess passed the 10 percent mark a long time ago."

Giving is a true indicator of our heart. Giving is a true indicator of the type of church member God has called us to be.

## The Cheerful Factor

The apostle Paul messes with my mind at times. Don't get me wrong. I mean that in a good and humble way. But his directness in Scripture can be unsettling and convicting. Then again, that's how the Holy Spirit uses Scripture.

So Paul was writing to the church at Corinth about giving. The Corinthian church was a troubled congregation in many ways. Paul wanted to make certain they were clear on this matter of stewardship.

First, he tells the church that their spiritual growth will be in direct relationship to their generous giving: "Remember this: The person who sows sparingly will also reap sparingly, and the person who sows generously will also reap generously" (2 Cor. 9:6). He left no doubt about the matter. He told the Corinthian church members they could not grow as Christians unless they were giving generously.

That truth for the church at Corinth is truth for us today in our churches.

But Paul does not stop there. Read these words from 2 Corinthians 9:7 carefully: "Each person should do as he has decided in his heart—not reluctantly or out of necessity, for God loves a cheerful giver."

First, Paul tells the church members the motivations they should not have as givers. They should not give with a reluctant motivation. If they are trying to hold on to something as they are trying to let go, they are reluctant givers. Those who give should do so with great willingness and total abandon.

Second, the apostle said we should not give out of the motivation of legalism. He calls it "out of necessity." We do not give to please a person or a set of guidelines. We give to please God. And in doing so, we find our greatest joy in giving. Those who give out of legalistic obligations will soon resent those guidelines.

But it's where Paul addresses the positive motive for giving that might present a greater challenge to some church members. He said we should be a *cheerful* giver. In fact, he is more emphatic than that. He says God loves a cheerful giver.

The Greek word for *cheerful* is the same word from which we get *hilarious*. This word is only used once in Scripture, in 2 Corinthians 9:7. The word connotes overflowing giving, joyous giving, and even hilarious giving. Giving should be one of the greatest joys of our lives. Giving with any other motive is not the type of giving God loves.

Church members should give. Church members should give joyously and with abandon. Church members should give, not because they are checking off a legalistic list, but because they find true joy in serving God in this way.

## The Action Plan

What, then, are some practical steps for church members? How do we proceed down the obedient path of giving?

The first obvious step is to make it a matter of prayer. Paul says in 2 Corinthians 9:7, "Each person should do as he has decided in his heart." Our "heart" is our relationship with God. Giving is a powerful but personal expression of how God has led us; that is how we decide in our heart.

Second, understand that the God we serve is not a God of limited resources. He is the God who created and can still create unlimited resources. Paul makes it clear that as we sow generously, we will reap generously. He does not say how God will do that, but he makes it clear that God has no limitations.

Often we approach stewardship from our limited perspective of resources. We therefore conclude that we can only give what we see. While we are certainly not to take unwise or foolish steps, most of us limit our giving by what we think is possible, not what God would have us give.

Finally, just do it. Just give. Give beyond your own comfort zone. Give as if God is really in charge of all we own and have.

And give without hesitation. Don't give begrudgingly. There is no person to whom you give who is perfect. There is no organization to which you give that is perfect. There is no church to which you give is perfect. Give without reservation. God will take care of the rest.

Your obedience to God is directly related to your giving.

Your faithfulness as a church member is a function of your giving.

And your joy as a believer in Christ is closely tied to your giving.

Be willing. Be cheerful.

And as you are considering the matter of stewardship in how and what you give to your church, be willing to make this statement without hesitation and with great joy.

I will give.

## *Points to Ponder*

1. Why have some church members developed a consumer mind-set of the church? How does that affect their giving to the church?

2. What are some of the ways you would describe a cheerful giver as Paul writes in 2 Corinthians 9:7?

3. Note several key points on money and generosity as Jesus notes in His Sermon on the Mount in Matthew 6:19–24.

4. Why should giving be motivated by a willing desire rather than legalistic guidelines? How would Jesus answer this question?

# Chapter 7

# I Will Not Be a Church Dropout

I have a "who's who" in my life.

They are the people who have been the greatest influence on me. They are friends. They are mentors. And they are family members. At the risk of omission, let me name a few.

There is my wife, Nellie Jo. She is one of the most godly and sacrificial people I know. It seems like every time she says something or does something, it is for the benefit of someone else. She rarely puts herself first.

Then there is my high school football coach, Joe Hendrickson. He shared the gospel with me in a Fellowship of Christian Athletes meeting. I trusted Christ as my Savior just a few hours after that meeting.[1]

And there are my three sons. Sam Rainer has taught me how to love a community with the gospel. Art Rainer has taught me what Christian loyalty looks like. And Jess

---

1. As an aside, I had a reunion with Coach Joe in late 2014. I had not seen him in over four decades. I was able to thank him and honor him and his family.

Rainer has been a model of Christian compassion for me to follow. And all three sons have taught me so much about being a Christian husband and father.

Lewis Drummond was my mentor who gave me a fire and passion for evangelism. Though he is with the Lord, his influence in my life remains strong,

Of course, my uncle, Jess Keller, would have to be on this list. From the previous chapter you know that he was a role model for me in generosity and giving.

Then there is Bob.

At least that is what I called him in an earlier book, *I Am a Church Member*.

The reason I did not give his full name in that book was simple. I did not get permission from Bob's family to write about him, and Bob died a few years ago.

Well, Bob's "secret" identity did not last long. There were too many people who knew Bob and knew his great character. And some people knew that Bob and I had crossed paths many years ago. It wasn't long before I was hearing from people: "That's Bob Hand you are talking about. That's just like Bob."

So here is the abbreviated story about Bob Hand.

I was a young man in my twenties. I had been married to Nellie Jo a few years, and we had two small sons at home. Jess was not yet born. I was a banker then, continuing a tradition in my family that lasted six generations.

When Nellie Jo and I joined the Golden Springs Baptist Church in Anniston, Alabama, I was ready to get involved. You see, I had been out of church for many years. When we joined the church, Nellie Jo was pregnant with our first child. I really wanted to get involved. And so I did.

Bob was watching me closely. He saw my youthful enthusiasm. He saw me become a father first of one son, then a second. And he was worried about me. He had seen it before.

Someone comes into the church and moves from no involvement to almost total immersion in church life. They are doing so many things that their family suffers. These enthusiastic church members begin to see the not-so-perfect side of church life the more they get involved. They get discouraged. And then they get tired.

They usually quit. Dropout. They become another church statistic.

They are called "comet Christians." They come in like a burning flame, only to disappear after a short while.

Bob Hand saw that happening to me. He took me under his guidance. He never lectured to me. He never spoke down to me. He told me stories. Those stories became my guide away from burnout and disillusionment.

I know that God used Bob to keep me on a trajectory that would ultimately take me to seminary and vocational ministry. Without Bob, I could have become another church dropout.

## The Burnout Syndrome

There have been a lot of studies about church dropouts. They tell similar stories. People leave churches for a number of reasons, but they are typically repeated. Someone hurts their feelings. They have no opportunities to serve. Or they are serving in so many places, that they are getting worn out and resentful of others who aren't serving. There are many other common stories.

A common thread runs through most of the stories. There is something about the church that brings big disappointment and disillusionment.

Burnout can occur when a church member is doing too much. Or too little. Or it can take place when a church member is doing things for which he or she has no passion.

*I Will* is not a checklist of things to do to please God or to be a good church member. This book is an expression of a natural overflow of ministry that should take place because of our love of Christ and His church. We will look at that issue in more depth in chapter 9.

For now, let's focus on those factors most likely to prevent church burnout. We have an abundance of research on church dropouts that will guide us in this direction.

There is obviously a reason every chapter and verse of the Bible is there. The Holy Spirit led the writers of Scripture, and those chapters and verses of the Bible are now in our canon.

For some, there may seem to be a tension between grace and works. We could do a lifetime study of that issue, but let's take an abbreviated overview for now.

One of the most quoted passages of the Bible is Ephesians 2:8–9: "For you are saved by grace through faith, and this not from yourselves; it is God's gift—not from works, so that no one can boast."

The verses are abundantly clear. Our salvation comes by grace, the unmerited favor we receive from God through our faith in Christ. Paul, the writer of this book, does not stop there. He not only tells us how we are saved; he tells how we are not saved. Our salvation, he says, does not come from ourselves or from our works.

Got that? Works do not save us.

But we can't end the passage there. Verse 10 is a critical part of this thought: "For we are His creation, created in Christ Jesus for good works, which God prepared ahead of time so that we should walk in them."

Read the entirety of Ephesians 2:8–10. We are not saved by works. But we are saved to do good works. And this last phrase is key: ". . . which God prepared ahead of time so that we should walk in them."

You see, God already has a plan for our service, our plan for our works in the church and beyond. Our salvation is free and unmerited; but that salvation should result in our works for Him.

So what do these verses have to do with church burnout?

We burn out when our motivation to do works is for anyone else but God. Let me return to my story of Bob Hand to illustrate.

Bob saw that I was saying "yes" to everyone in the church. I was a deacon. I was a Sunday school teacher. I was a boys' mission leader. I taught a first grade training class. I was in a 5:00 a.m. prayer group. I led a Saturday church work crew. I served on three committees. I was an usher.

You get the picture.

None of those ministries were bad choices. I just had said "yes" to everyone. I got to the point where I was doing so many things that I was doing none well.

Bob intervened. In his own gentle way, he told me stories. Those stories pointed to my motivations for ministry in the church. I'm slow; but I finally got it. My motivation for what I was doing was primarily to please people. My pastor asked me to lead the missions group. A good friend asked me to teach the Sunday school class. A church member who was my bank customer asked me to be in the morning prayer groups.

All were good ministries. All had incredible purposes. But my motivations were not always right. I was more of a people pleaser than a God pleaser.

Look at Ephesians 2:10 again: "For we are His creation, created in Christ Jesus for good works, which God prepared ahead of time so that we should walk in them."

The "good works" that we are to do are those that God has prepared. Those are places where we should "walk." We are to serve as God has showed us. We are to please Him. Our motive is to glorify Him, serve Him, and please Him. If we do that, we will serve gladly and never burn out.

Of course, volumes have been written on how we should serve God in our church. Resources on spiritual gifts, in particular, are invaluable to help us understand our passions and giftedness for service.

For now, we will focus on this simple truth. Church burn-out will not take place if we are seeking to please God in our service rather than to please people.

## The Ministry Atrophy Factor

While burnout can lead to our dropping out of church, even a greater factor is ministry atrophy. The word *atrophy* has as its primary meaning the biological reality that our organs and tissue will waste away if we don't use them.

Though it's been many years, I remember vividly the first year I played high school football. The previous May I suffered a compound fracture in my leg from falling off a horse. The cast was finally removed in mid-July, just three weeks before football practice began. You can probably anticipate the rest of the story. I tried to practice contact football with a leg that had not been in use for more than two months. I was pathetic. The muscles in my leg were of little use. They had atrophied.

In the same sense, our "spiritual muscles" atrophy when we don't use them. While we don't serve in our churches because of a legalistic checklist, we are still to serve. When Paul wrote Ephesians, he was writing to a specific church in Ephesus. He wanted to remind the Ephesian church members of their salvation by grace through faith. But he was also clear that our response to grace is works in His power.

Please allow me to be blunt here. If you are not serving in your church, you are not a legitimate church member. When Paul wrote to the church in Corinth, he spoke of how we must serve the body of Christ through the metaphor of "members."

Remember Paul's words in 1 Corinthians 12:27: "Now you are the body of Christ, and individual members of it." Earlier Paul gave names to these parts or members of the body: the eye, the ear, the hand, and the feet. His point is crystal clear. If a member is not functioning, it is of no use to the body.

If you are a church member who is not functioning or serving, you are of no use to the body. Your ministry is atrophying.

I can anticipate some objections to this statement. I have heard them before. Let me summarize them with a series of e-mail exchanges I had with a friend. She wrote me that she had concluded she would drop out of church life. She tried to find places of service, but she met numerous roadblocks because she was a relatively new member. She was, as she said it "outside the circle of influence." Simply put, longer-term members did not ask her to serve at all.

I won't bore you with all the details of our e-mail exchange. I will simply quote her final e-mail to me. It was indeed a happy ending.

"While it's true no one in the church was asking me to serve," she wrote, "that was only a convenient excuse for me. I decided to start my own personal prayer ministry for church members. I took the church directory every day and starting praying for church members and church staff by name."

Her e-mail continued,

"I then began volunteering for a few opportunities where someone would offer a generic invitation. I was selective in choosing those areas that really excited me. Obviously, some of the longer-term church members began to notice me and my work. I now have more opportunities for service than I can accept."

Her final words are poignant:

"I was about to become a church dropout. But my reasons were rooted in my pride because no one was asking me to serve. I learned that I can pray without being asked, and I can serve without being asked. I'm glad I decided to put my foolish pride aside, and seek to serve in ways I knew I could."

## The Crux of the Matter

Most church dropouts take place for one of two reasons. One, church members become overcommitted and burn out. They are the comet Christians who come in a flame, but quickly disappear. Two, some church members do not serve at all for a variety of reasons. They haven't been asked to serve. They are comfortable with their spectator status. Or they may not really be a believer in Christ.

Either extreme is wrong. Legalistic works in the church have the wrong motives. Failure to serve has the wrong actions.

A few months ago, I received this comment on my blog. It was from a lady who insisted that church ministry through the local church is over-emphasized. Here are her comments directly from the blog:

> "If anyone thinks you need to do something under the auspices of a local congregation (or even the national/global offices of a denomination) to be doing the work of God, that person has lived an extremely sheltered life–or they are extremely and willfully blind/stupid. 99.99% of God's work is happening without ANY input from churches. Demanding that the people who do that work (and it is tough, energy-sapping work) give precious time to church 'ministries' and small groups will drive those people away. This kind of thinking is at least partially responsible for the rise of the Nones and Dones. Time to take responsibility for that."

I agree with her in the sense that much good ministry is taking place in areas other than local churches. But I respectfully and passionately disagree that the local church is not key in God's plan for ministry. The great majority of the New Testament was either written to a local church or in the context of local churches.

The crux of the matter is this: We are to avoid the extremes that lead to church dropout, either through legalistic over-commitment or intentional non-commitment.

We are indeed to serve. We are indeed to function as a member of the body of Christ. And we are to do so in a way that pleases God before people.

An inactive church member is an oxymoron. A church dropout is a disobedient Christian. May we now make this commitment:

I will not be a church dropout.

## *Points to Ponder*

1. Relate spiritual atrophy to Paul's metaphor of being a member of the body of Christ in 1 Corinthians 12.

2. Explain the connection between grace and works in Ephesians 2:8–10.

3. What have your observations told you about the reason church members drop out of the church?

4. Compare and contrast over-commitment and atrophy in the context of local church ministry and service.

# Chapter 8

# I Will Avoid the Traps of Churchianity

I know. *Churchianity* is not a word. I think it should be. I would define it as: "practicing our church and religious beliefs according to human standards rather than biblical guidelines."

You see, in many of our churches we are redefining church membership to be something different than the sacrificial and functional teachings of 1 Corinthians 12. As a consequence, too many church members are really practicing churchianity instead of vibrant Christianity.

Look at that chapter. Look at its implications. Look specifically at 1 Corinthians 12:27–28. "Now you are the body of Christ, and individual members of it. And God has placed these in the church."

Do you see that? Do you see what biblical church membership really is? Members of the church comprise the whole and are essential parts of it. The apostle Paul uses the body metaphor to explain that church members are parts of the body. Some are ears; others are eyes. Some are feet; still others are hands. That is why he concludes: "For as the body is one and has many parts, and all the parts of that body, though many, are one body—so also is Christ" (1 Cor. 12:12).

So, as church members, we are to function. We are to sacrifice. We are to practice vibrant Christianity instead of churchianity. The former is biblical and self-giving. The latter is unbiblical and self-serving.

How did we get to where we are today? This book is too brief to review the decline of healthy church life, particularly in the U.S. Instead, I will share five major symptoms of churchianity, symptoms we must completely avoid.

## Symptom #1: Church Is a Spectator Sport

Those who know me know I am a college football fan. I guess I am a pretty rabid college football fan as well. Instead of drawing the ire of fans of other schools, I will simply say that my team is pretty good. Indeed, their record in recent years is one of the best in the sport.

So it is with a bit of amusement I sit in the stands during a game and hear our fans scream out what the team should or shouldn't do, or what the coach should or shouldn't do. At other times, I go to the online bulletin board for my team. Again, I read how our fans often know so much more than the coaches and the players.

But I have to admit, I am guilty at times myself. If we are not attending a game, my son, Jess, and I typically watch the game on television in our respective homes. Looking at our texts after the game is over can be an amusing exercise. We knew exactly what play should be called. We knew what mistakes the coaches were making.

Yeah right. We are really smarter at football than those coaches and players. Not.

We participate in the sport as a spectator. We don't participate in the grueling practices. We don't have the knowledge and experience of the coaches. We don't experience the pressure of fans, administrators, recruiting, and winning.

We sit back and watch and offer our "valuable" input.

Churchianity can be like a spectator sport. Members attend but they don't actively participate. They expect others to do ministry. For some, the only time they get passionate is at a church business meeting where they express their displeasure and anger.

This story is not prescriptive, but it does make a point. A pastor walked into the room where he knew a tense business meeting was waiting. He spoke right before the meeting was called to order. It is my understanding that he said something like this: "Welcome to our business meeting, folks! Before we get started, let's have a time of sharing. Someone share with the group how you have shared the gospel of Christ this past month."

Silence.

Not one person responded. It appeared that not one person had been a gospel witness. The pastor did not have to say anything else. It is easy to be a complainer and a spectator. But we cannot treat our churches like spectator sports.

By the way, the business meeting was not nearly as rancorous as many had expected.

## Symptom #2: Church Is about Me

This subject, "church is about me," was really a major sub-theme of my earlier book, *I Am a Church Member*. That book focused on the attitudes of church members. This book, of course, focuses on the actions of church members. Specifically, we have been looking for ways to move church members toward an outward focus.

When we have a country club mentality about the church, we do not serve. Instead, we seek to be served. We have paid our "dues," so we expect others to work for us. What are some signs that a church member has the symptom of "church is about me"? These statements are indicative:

- "I told the pastor what I wanted him to preach; he just doesn't listen to me."
- "I don't like the temperature in the worship center."
- "If we don't change our music style, I'm not coming back. I'll find another church that can meet my needs."
- "Someone is in our seat/pew."
- "The church decided not to offer the 7:30 a.m. service anymore because only a few people are attending. Well, that's my service. If it's gone, so am I."
- "The pastor did not visit my sister's mother-in-law in the hospital, even though I told him to."
- "The church voted to paint the worship center a hideous color. I am infuriated. I just might stop giving."

You get the picture. Biblical church life is about serving, about sacrificing, about giving, and about putting others before our own desires and needs. Churchianity is about being served, receiving, getting your way, and insisting on your needs and wants before others.

## Symptom #3: Church Is about Dwelling on Its Flaws

Do you remember my story about Bob Hand? Bob was my informal mentor when I was a twenty-something banker. I noted that he became concerned about me because I was acting like a comet Christian. I was saying "yes" to everything and everyone.

But I think his concern hit a new level when I started complaining about some things in the church. He knew that was a symptom of churchianity, thought he wouldn't phrase it that way.

So Bob did what he did best. He told me a story. He told me a story about marriage, and how in the early days of the marriage both the husband and the wife can see no wrong in each other. But then, after living together a while, each of them begins to notice the other one is not perfect.

Bob told me that story happens in every marriage. And we basically have one of two choices. We can try to see the best in our spouse and love him or her despite the imperfections (he said it's that "for better or worse" thing). Or we can complain and nag about the shortcomings. Maybe to the point of separation. Maybe to the point of divorce.

He then asked me the rhetorical question as he always did: What's the better choice?

The story hit home. I knew Bob was referring to my relationship with the church where we were members. It was a good lesson. I started praying more for leaders and members in my church rather than complaining about them.

No, they weren't perfect. But, then again, neither am I.

We shouldn't act surprised when we find imperfections in the churches where we are members. That reality goes all the way back to the first Christian churches. You can find their stories in the New Testament. For example, let's look at one church in the New Testament, the Corinthian church, focusing on 1 Corinthians only. Here is a sample of some of the issues they faced:

- Church members had cliques and had formed personality cults.
- There was a significant amount of carnal behavior.
- Church members and leaders did not deal with sexual immorality and sexual perversion in the church.
- There was a significant level of worldliness and materialism.
- Church members were taking one another to court.
- There was rebellion against apostolic authority.
- The church did not discipline members who had fallen into sin.
- There was a misunderstanding about spiritual gifts.
- There were abuses of the Lord's Supper.

- There were abuses of liberty.
- The church was dealing with heresies concerning the resurrection.

And you thought your church had problems.

The gospel is the story of what God did for us through His Son Jesus. The gospel is about salvation by grace through faith. The gospel is about Jesus dying on a cross. He is our substitute. He became sin. He took on our sin and took our punishment for us.

The gospel is John 3:16, how much God loved us. It is about the Father sacrificing the Son for a bunch of sinful and disobedient people.

Like me. And you.

So how do we respond to that gift? How do we demonstrate that we, as a people who have received grace, can demonstrate grace toward others in the church?

Frankly, we don't do so well at times.

We become critical of the pastor and staff. We don't like what the elders or deacons are doing. We don't like the music chosen by the worship leader. We are critical of the children's minister.

Such attitudes and behaviors are symptomatic of churchianity, not biblical church membership. You can be assured that your church is not perfect. You can be certain that your pastor and church staff are not perfect. And there is no doubt that you will find a lot of messed up sinners in your church. Indeed we are among them.

We have a real choice. We can practice churchianity and dwell on the flaws and be critical. Or we can practice biblical church membership and extend grace toward others.

After all, without the grace of our Lord Jesus Christ, we would have no hope ourselves.

## Symptom #4: Church Has Low Expectations

Joanna became a member of Franklin Community Church a little over a year ago. She liked the preaching and the music. It was a convenient drive from her house to the church. The children's ministry was outstanding. Indeed, that was the greatest draw to the church since she had two children ages seven and nine. She felt responsible for their spiritual nurturing since her husband did not attend church.

So Joanna made the decision to join FCC. There was a card in the church bulletin that allowed her to show her interest in church membership. She wrote her name, address, and e-mail address. And she waited.

She did not hear from the church for six weeks. She was preparing to call the church office to find out what was taking place. That week, however, she received a letter from the church: "Dear Joanna. We are pleased to inform you that you were voted to be a member of the church in our most recent monthly business meeting. Welcome to Franklin Community Church!"

That was it?

No one from the church had ever contacted her. No one knows if she is really a Christian or not. No one has shared with her information about the church. No one has indicated to her how she might best serve in the church.

Yes, that was it.

Joanna knew from her childhood that many churches required people to "walk the aisle" and complete a membership card. They were then presented to the church on the spot, even if no one knew them. On some occasions they would be voted for membership subsequently in a church business meeting.

Still, she was surprised that churches still have such low expectations of its members. So she tried sticking with the church for over a year. During that time, no one contacted her. No one asked her to serve. No one told her anything about the church.

Joanna admits she could have done a better job initiating contact with church leaders. But the whole environment of the church was so "low expectation" that she just was not motivated to do so.

With so few expectations of her, Joanna never really got connected. She started attending less frequently. Still no one contacted her. Soon she and her children left the church altogether. No one missed them. No one contacted them.

For Joanna and her children, the story has a happy ending. She got involved in another church. People contacted her. She was happy to go through a new members' class for membership in the church. And she was immediately given the opportunity to connect with a small group and to be involved in ministry. She and the kids are doing well.

As a closing thought, I asked her if Franklin Community Church *never* really contacted her in any way. She paused for a moment and then said: "There was one piece of communication from the church I received right after I was notified I had been accepted into membership. They sent me a box of offering envelopes."

This story vividly illustrates a church with low expectations practicing churchianity. Note some of the characteristics of the low expectation church:

- They don't have a new members' class. This entry point is critical to provide new and prospective members both information on the church and expectations of the members.
- They don't move members to a small group or Sunday school class. This group is vital for members to develop relationships and to become more involved in church life.
- They don't move members toward involvement in ministry. Such a move communicates that members are first to serve others.
- There is little communication from the church to the members. In the illustration, Franklin Community Church sent two pieces of information in a year: a membership letter and a box of offering envelopes.

Churches with low expectations have more members who practice churchianity. Sadly, there are too many low expectation churches today.

## Symptom #5: Church Has Cliquish Membership

This symptom is similar to #4 in that it's difficult to get involved in the church. One church has only a few members involved because it is a low expectation church. Another church had few members involved because most members aren't connected with key cliques in the church.

The cliques can take different forms. One common clique is an informal power group in the church. They represent an informal alliance of typically longer-term members. In many ways, they consider the church "my church." Anyone has to get tacit approval from that group to get involved or to get anything accomplished.

Another clique can be a family power group. Some older churches especially have a network of connected people whose origin is one or two families. Those families may date back to the birth of the church.

Sometimes the clique may be a formal group such as the elders or deacons or church council. Of course most of these groups are healthy and functioning biblically. But if the group becomes a barrier to members becoming meaningfully involved in the church, the members are practicing churchianity. They are hindered from functioning as biblical church members.

## The Two Big Sources of Churchianity

A church whose members practice churchianity typically have two major causative factors. Church members are first precluded from functioning as biblical church members. The barriers may be institutional or attitudinal. There could be formal structures in place that hinder meaningful involvement. Or there could simply be the traditionalist response of: "We've never done it that way before." Second, some church members make a choice not to function as biblical church members, and they are at least tacitly allowed to pursue that path.

Both are wrong.

Both are unbiblical expressions of churchianity.

Let us look at how we function in our churches. Is it biblical or is it a form of churchianity? If it is the latter, may we make a renewed commitment? If we are asked if we will continue to practice churchianity, let us respond without hesitation.

I will not.

## *Points to Ponder*

1.  Thumb through 1 Corinthians and find at least five examples where the church was having problems. Make sure you describe the problems and note the chapter and verses.

2.  What are some characteristics of a church that has become a spectator sport for most of its members?

3.  Why do some power groups form in a church? What are some of the consequences of these power groups?

4.  What personal commitment should you make as a church member not to practice churchianity?

## Chapter 9

# I Will Make a Difference

**H**is name was Jeremiah Lanphier. The date was September 23, 1857. The location was New York City.

For days Lanphier had been handing out flyers about a time of prayer. He likely distributed more than twenty thousand flyers by himself.

He was a man under God's conviction. He was desperate for a move of God, and he knew no human-powered system or organization could manufacture such a move.

So he prayed. And he called others to prayer as well.

Lanphier probably had great anticipation that many would show up at noon on September 27. The city had a population of one million. His flyers were likely seen by more than the original twenty thousand recipients of the flyers.

So he went to the borrowed upper room of a church and prayed and waited. For thirty minutes no one showed up. Then he heard the footsteps of a few coming to the prayer meeting. Six other people joined him.

Their numbers increased to fourteen the next week. Then twenty-three the next week. And the prayer meetings continued to grow.

The presence of God was so powerful. Those who were in the meetings decided to have the gatherings every day. And the numbers continued to increase. By winter of 1857 the prayer meetings were filling three large churches every day. Then, by March of 1858, every available public hall and church in New York City was filled every day.

Horace Greeley, the famous newspaper editor, sent a reporter to attempt to count the numbers at these meetings. He could only make it to six locations by horse and buggy in that one-hour period. He still counted sixty-one hundred people.

The prayer movement spread across the nation. At one season of this movement, ten thousand people were becoming believers each week. More than one scholar has estimated that one million people became followers of Christ through these prayer meetings.

A movement had begun.

Today I am praying for another movement of God.

## A Movement Where People Say "I Will"

I am concerned about our churches. I am not alone.

I won't bore you with more dire statistics about the state of American congregations. Suffice it to say, it's not a pretty picture.

The problem is not the institutional church. The problem is not denominations. The problem is me. And you.

Denominations are no stronger than their churches. And churches are no stronger than their church members. I am a church member. The problem begins with me and with you.

Jeremiah Lanphier was just one person, just like you and me. He knew he could not create a movement. His role was to petition to God for Him to move. His role was to be willing. To be willing to say, "I will."

So God used one obedient nobody and began a movement.

It is time to stop placing the blame elsewhere. It is time to look into the mirror and ask God where we can say, "I will."

Notice how God brings movements back to His churches. He did with Jeremiah Lanphier. He did with the New Testament churches.

We are members of our respective churches. We are responsible. Is it possible, through us, God will start a movement?

While we cannot manufacture a movement, we can do what Jeremiah Lanphier did. He was obedient. It's that simple and that profound. He was obedient.

It is time to become those types of obedient church members in our congregations. It is time to take 1 Corinthians 12 seriously and be a vital part of the body of Christ.

It is time to say, "I will."

*I will have the attitude of Christ and put other church members before my wants and desires.*

*I will gladly participate in corporate worship with my fellow church members as long as I am physically able.*

*I will get involved in a group or a class so that I might grow spiritually together with others, and so that I might be accountable to them.*

*I will go and share the gospel with others in words and deeds, and not be ashamed of my Savior.*

*I will give abundantly and joyfully, recognizing that God is the owner of all things I currently steward.*

*I will participate in the life of my church because God leads me to do so, not because I feel compelled to please people and overcommit.*

*I will focus on what Christ has done for me, and not on the flaws of my church, its leaders, or its members.*

*And I will pray that God will use me as an instrument to revive His church, for His name, and for His glory.*

## One Concluding Thought

A few years ago I found myself in the hospital waiting room with my wife and the parents of my daughter-in-law. We had been told that it did not look good, but I still prayed for a miracle.

When my son, Jess, came into the room, I knew. He did not speak a word. But I knew.

His son, Will, had died. My grandson was with the Lord.

Jess fell on my shoulders. We both began to cry.

How does a dad console his son who just lost a son? What words could I possibly say to comfort him? My words were broken and soft, but I spoke, "Jess, what can I do for you?"

Jess spoke.

They are words that are etched into my memory for as long as I live. Jess said, "Dad, please pray that God will use Will's life and death to bring glory to His name wherever I go."

That was it.

His request was not about him. It was not about his needs and his wants. It was about using a tragic event to bring glory to God.

My response was simple: "I will."

It is time.

It is time for church members to become a part of a movement where self is sacrificed and the body of Christ is strengthened. It is time to seek to bring glory to God through His church. It is time for a real revival of the hearts of church members.

So, beginning this moment, become the type of church member who will be used by God to be an instrument of a movement of revival in our churches. Listen to Him carefully. Follow Him obediently.

And when He speaks to move us to action, be willing to say without reservation or hesitation:

I will make a difference.

## *Points to Ponder*

1. What can we learn from the life of Jeremiah Lanphier to be the type of church members God wants us to be?

2. Give your best description of what a 1 Corinthians 12 church member looks like.

3. What does it mean to be a self-sacrificial church member?

4. How has this book changed you in your own approach to church membership? How has it made you more outwardly focused?.

## Appendix

# A Commitment to "I Will"

### To be read individually or responsively

I will have the attitude of Christ and put other church members before my wants and desires.

*I will.*

I will gladly participate in corporate worship with my fellow church members as long as I am physically able.

*I will.*

I will get involved in a group or a class so that I might grow spiritually together with others, and so that I might be accountable to them.

*I will.*

I will go and share the gospel with others in words and deeds and not be ashamed of my Savior.

*I will.*

I will give abundantly and joyfully, recognizing that God is the owner of all things I currently steward.

*I will.*

I will participate in the life of my church because God leads me to do so, not because I feel compelled to please people or to feel guilty for saying "no."

*I will.*

I will focus on the positive ways God is using my church, and not on the flaws of my church, its leaders, or its members.

*I will.*

And I will pray that God will use me as an instrument to revive His church, for His name, and for His glory.

*I will.*

---

*Sign and Date*